Money of the
American Indians

Ancient Mexican currencies as depicted in Aztec glyphs, from the *Codex Mendoza.* 1) Cotton mantle, as worn by a noble; 2) Preparation of quetzal feathers; 3) A packet of the feathers; 4) A bowl of gold granules; 5) Goldsmiths preparing gold disc; 6) Lapidary showing an apprentice how to fashion jade beads; 7) a string of jade beads, of alternating oblong and round shape; 8) A bundle of cacao beans; 9) Copper bells, a Mayan currency; 10) rude depiction of copper axe or hatchet; 11) Copper hatchet blade. Although the hatchet does not seem to have progressed beyond the status of a favorite barter item, the blade is thought to have served as a prototype for an early post-Columbian currency which circulated in Oaxaca.

Money of the
American Indians

and Other Primitive Currencies
of the Americas

Don Taxay

NUMMUS PRESS

New York

Published by Nummus Press
Box 1058, Flushing, N. Y. 11355

Copyright © Don Taxay, 1970

Library of Congress Catalog Number 78-141349

ISBN 0-87841-001-5

Printed in the United States of America

To Dadaji and Didiji

Contents

Foreword 9

Introduction 13

PART I

MEXICO, AND CENTRAL AND SOUTH AMERICA

1. Origins 27
2. Cloth, Feathers and Gold 29
3. Jade 37
4. Other Early Mexican and Central
   American Currencies 41
5. The Mysterious Money of the Amazons
   and Other Carib and Arawak Currencies 48
6. Recent Currencies of Central America 53
7. Other Currencies of South America 56
8. The Lesser Antilles 61

PART II

NORTH AMERICA

9. California 65
10. The Northwest Coast 88
11. Moving Eastward 104
12. Roanoke and Wampum 107
13. Wampum in Dress and Ceremony 119
14. Wampum—Its Manufacture and Currency Use 131
15. North American Colonial Currencies 145

Sources Cited 149

Index 155

Foreword

The subject of American Indian currency, and related numismatic questions, has long received a one-sided consideration. All too often it has been approached by anthropologists who have tended to read into the trade objects they encounter a quasi-currency status, as against the restrictive definitions which a scholar immersed in the requirements of numismatic usage would demand. On the other hand, the latter, equally unaware of the subtle concepts which often attend barter, refuses to attribute numismatic credence to what he regards as a simple trade object.

It is refreshing, then, to read a work in which a conscientious effort has been made to intertwine both concepts. Based upon his long-time experience as a numismatist, the author has delved deeply into anthropological literature to gain an understanding of the several areas discussed, and he has succeeded in presenting a broad reflection of aboriginal currency. He has not only considered the strictly technological and economic aspects of the subject, but is aware of the social implications as well and—what is most important to this writer—the religio-mythic areas of involvement. It is this latter character which often has a far greater implication in Indian life than many scholarly writers understand; barter is not only a matter of exchange of goods—it involves many other aspects of interchange in aboriginal life. Mr. Taxay thoroughly understands this fact, and builds many of his theories upon it.

Thus, while one might occasionally question a specific, the over-all treatment of the subject is eminently sound, and it is felt that the present work will introduce the reader to many areas heretofore inadequately studied.

We are pleased to have been able to cooperate in providing specimens of American Indian currency for inclusion in this work, and it is hoped that the result will serve as a useful reference volume for all those interested in the subject.

Frederick J. Dockstader
Director, Museum of the American Indian,
New York City
Oct., 1970
Heye Foundation

9

ACKNOWLEDGMENTS

As a rule, the completion of a new work finds me indebted to a good many persons and institutions for assistance of various kinds. The present occasion is rather exceptional in that my debts, though not less deep, are owed almost entirely to Dr. Frederick Dockstader and the Museum of the American Indian, Heye Foundation. Dr. Dockstader took considerable time out of his very busy schedule not only to critically read the manuscript (for which it is much improved), but to grace it with a foreword. For the majority of my photographic prints, also, I must thank the Museum of the American Indian. Other sources, to whom, of course, I am likewise grateful, are the Chase Manhattan Bank Money Museum, the New York Public Library, the U.S. Bureau of Ethnology, the Peabody Museum, Harvard University, and the Hudson Historical Bureau. Finally, for permission to reproduce certain of the quotations that appear in this work, I want to thank the Peabody Museum, the Carnegie Institution of Washington, the University of Chicago Press, Penguin Books, Ltd. of Middlesex, Farrar, Straus & Giroux, Inc. of New York City, and the New American Library of World Literature, Inc. (Mentor Books) of New York City.

D.T.
August, 1970

Introduction

Whatever else it may be, money is a medium which we use, by common consent, to pay for goods and services. By contrast, barter involves the consent of only the participants. An article may thus be acceptable in one instance and not in another.

Over a period of time, certain barter items tend to become more popular than others, and so acquire a greater acceptability in exchange. Eventually, through the stabilizing force of custom, the former may even take on the equivalent of a legal tender status, becoming, in effect, money. The rule then is clear enough, and it is only due to its scrupulous disregard that extreme statements so often appear with respect to this or that article or group of articles.

Not a little confusion has been caused by overzealous authors trying to extend their citations, and merchants their numismatic stock. These practices have, in effect, given rise to a new form of currency "debasement," wherein various favored (and even not so favored) barter items are pawned off on the uninitiated as primitive money.

Against this undue liberality, one finds the conservative ethnologist who virtually gainsays the existence of any money but our own coin and paper currency. Adherents of this view define money in terms of various criteria such as standardization, durability, portability, divisibility, stability and cognizability. What they fail to grasp is that, however useful these criteria might be for measuring the development of a currency, they have no direct bearing on its nature. We do not demand, by way of a definition, that a professor be intelligent, erudite, articulate and conscientious. To be sure, a good professor will be all these things—but then, are all professors good? Similarly, a currency need not be as sophisticated as our own to be a currency. It is function, not form, that matters. Moreover, even according to the foregoing criteria, primitive currencies are not, in all respects, inferior to our own. Most will outlast our dollar bills, and some have even greater durability than coins. Again, primitive currencies, like primitive societies, are peculiarly stable unless disturbed by some "civilizing" influence.* Much primitive money is as portable as coins and notes, though, admittedly, there are a few classic exceptions. Generally speaking, it is most vulnerable from the standpoint of standardization and cognizability. With few exceptions, primitive money will lack a stamp of authority to guarantee its value.

Money is a Neolithic invention. Before that time, life was essentially communalistic. The hunt required, for the most part, a coordinated effort, and whatever was killed was scrupulously shared. Moreover, Man's wanderings in pursuit of the herds** did not encourage him to accumulate goods, nor the elementary character of his needs promote individual specialization. Each family group was therefore economically self-sufficient. Even the eventual emergence of specialists in the form of shamans, artists, and artizans, did not, for a very long time, alter the economic pattern. They were still too few, and could thus be supported by the vast majority of homogeneous non-specialists.

Community specialization seems to have preceeded individual specialization as an economic factor. Distributed as they were over such a wide area, every group possessed certain goods that were desired by others. Even the Polar Eskimos, who were once thought to have lived for centuries in complete isolation and in ignorance of the outside world, were not destitute of inter-community trade.

Sometime around the fourth millenium B.C., the earliest American groups began to farm or, perhaps, fish at regular sites—in a word, to settle down. Situated on a coast, or by a lake or river, a group would parcel out its area to the clans or families of which it was composed. A growing sense of permanence, and thus of personal property, increased the initiative of the individual, created a broader specialization, and undermined the self-sufficiency of the family. At the same time, surpluses paved the way for barter.

Where individual property rights and specialization were developed conjointly, the result was large surpluses and wealth. Again, where a particular article was so favored that it eventually came to symbolize wealth, and was always accepted at an acknowledged value, money was born. Its role as a

---

* All too often in the form of a massive importation of counterfeits.

** This, however, should be qualified. So long as the ecology of an area remained stable, the hunters knew where and when to look for particular wildlife, which returned at the same time each year. Thus, while the hunters may have moved about, their movements were generally predictable, and were punctuated by a good deal of leisure.

medium of exchange followed inevitably, and was not, as endlessly repeated, due to a conscious decision on the part of early Man to facilitate trade.

A perusal of any representative collection of primitive money will reveal an overwhelming preponderance of shell ornaments, and, thereafter, of teeth, stones and feathers. There is probably no continent to which shell currency is foreign, including Europe, though the extinction of Paleolithic and Neolithic culture patterns there deprives us of a certainty. Ethnologists, concentrating on the cowry, call our attention to its widespread use as a fertility charm, which they attribute to its resemblance to the vaginal fold. This view, however, cannot be sustained in the face of an equally widespread use not only of other shells, but of pearls and jade for similar ritualistic and prophylactic purposes.

The true association by which these three articles have endeared themselves to our kind is rather with the sea, with water. That shells and pearls should remind us of water requires no explanation. To the ancients, the deep green color of jade was an equally forceful association. Thus, the latter was the most acceptable offering to the Chinese river god Ho Po, while the Mexican goddess of lakes, oceans and water was named Chalchiuhtlicue, or "She of the jade skirt."

Because shells, pearls and jade symbolized the sea, they embodied all the varied and profound significance Man attached to the latter. It was at once the infinite Void, the self-existent first cause, and the creative vitality that sustained life. This may be the reason why the figure of a shell is represented in the Mayan hieroglyph for zero, or completion. Certainly, there is no ambiguity concerning its use in the Cook Islands as a symbol of the self-existent universe. Again, the inhabitants of Nauru, just west of the Gilbert group, tell how the universe was created by the cosmic spider from a great conch shell, while those of the New Hebrides say that the mother of the human race sprang from a cowrie. In Raiatean legend, the Creator was at first concealed in an egg-shaped shell, and then, from its shards, formed the islands where men could dwell. In North America, the Haida told how the first people sprang from a shell, while, to the Omaha, it symbolized Wakonda, the Great Spirit. Gold discs, wrought by the Toltecs of Mexico, actually depict gods emerging from shells.

Because of the fertilizing effect of rain, it was natural that the shell should figure prominently as a fecunity charm. Here, the examples are almost inexhaustible. In East Africa, girls wear belts and aprons of cowries until after having their first child. In Pompeii, the shells were worn to prevent sterility. Among the Japanese and the Arapaho, a smooth shell is used to ease delivery. And so on.

Since death was regarded as a rebirth into another world, the rituals attending it were also accompanied by water symbols. In ancient China, jade, a pearl, or a shell (according to the rank of the individual) was placed in the mouth of the deceased, which had first been filled with rice. The Maya practised an almost identical ritual, placing a jade bead in the corpse's mouth after it had been filled with maize. Pearls have also been found in the mouths of skulls in the ancient Mississippi Valley.

By association, shells eventually became good luck charms with the broadest potencies. Their use as talismans has been noted in such varied places as Togo, Ceylon, India, Persia, California, Corfu, the Pacific Islands, Hungary, Norway, and the Middle East. Even in modern times, women, children and draft animals in Northern Arabia are said to wear shells to ward off the evil eye.

There is one other point to consider with reference to the magical properties of shells, and this involves their medicinal role among the hunting tribes of the Arctic, Sub-Arctic and Plains regions. At first blush, it would appear that healing potencies would be a natural extension of the properties already ascribed through an association with water. Here, however, we must seek for a different explanation. To begin with, Northern Paleolithic people, exposed as they are to severe weather, tend to apotheosize the wind above all else. Jubmel, the Lapp deity, was thus once a wind god. The Eskimos, in a similar way, call the Supreme Existence Sillam Innua, "the owner of the winds." A peculiar significance arises due to a connection with the cowrie, which the Eskimos consider to be the oldest of all healing amulets. The name they give to it—*iteg*, or "anus," derives from an association with the passing of wind, which, together with the breath is considered a potent force in healing.[1]

Another example might be taken from the Ojibwa, or their southern Algonquian and Siouan neighbors who have borrowed from them. These tribes maintain a sacred Midé, or medicine society, the founding of which is attributed, by the Ojibwa, to the divine Minabozho. Appropriately, the society is symbolized by a cowrie shell, while Minabozho is known as "the ruler of the winds," and represented by a hare, which is a widely recognized American Indian symbol for the air, or wind. During the Midé ritual, the shaman "swallows" some cowries, and conveys their healing power to a medicine bag by breathing on it. The bag is then pointed toward the patient, who is thought to be healed through the invisible emanation of power. Cowries are also used by these tribes in their initiation ceremony. Here the candidate will ostensibly die and be reborn, the cowrie supposedly entering his heart, and later emerging from his mouth.

Still another example may be found in the great Mexican deity Quetzalcoatl who was symbolized by the cross section of a conch shell. Quetzalcoatl enjoyed numerous divine aspects, and was the creator of Mankind in its last rebirth. However, it seems likely that the shell symbol relates to his important aspect as wind deity.

According to the evidence of archeology, our Paleolithic forefathers in Europe, and on the steppes of Russia, had already begun to take a keen interest in shells some twenty-five thousand years ago. Perhaps, because they roared when held to the ear, shells seemed to contain, at least for men living in more temperate zones, something of the sea. Farther north, the same phenomenon might be associated with the wind. That shells came from the sea, or, as large conches, could be blown, would also have seemed significant. Either way, they were endowed with magical potentialities, and, along with animal teeth and bone (the latter wrought into beads), which gave the wearer power over his prey, were made into necklaces, legbands and headdresses. It was no mere desire for self-adornment, but the serious business of survival that gave rise to this primeval jewelry. As time went on, the accretion of new associations, or extensions of the old, led to a wider employment of the shells, and their magical properties made them valuable in the sense that people required them for their well-being here and hereafter.*

Gradually, a rudimentary economy evolved, culminating in a medium of exchange. Pearls and jade were not so easily obtained, and thus remained a store of value, though the latter, as we shall see, was worked sufficiently in Mexico and South America to have a genuine currency function there. Teeth, with one exception, did not find a monetary use in America. This offers a marked contrast to the situation in Oceania, where, even within a predominantly agricultural pattern, the remnants of a hunting life have served to retain their old magical significance.

We have already discussed the water symbolism of jade, and could extend the same arguments in favor of crystal, which, in addition, was considered a powerful shamanizing tool. Yet, how shall we account for the monetary use of other, relatively common stones? Speaking generally, it may be said that *no* stone is so common that some resemblance, real or fancied, to an animal or

---

* In this they paralleled the early use of red ochre, which is among the most ancient of all known magical substances, and thus of human desiderata. Ochre apparently symbolized the blood, or life substance, of the earth, its use as a symbol of blood being, in fact, known from historical times. In view of the ubiquitous legend of Mankind emerging from the womb of the earth, the ancient use of ochre in burial was most likely to facilitate rebirth in the next world. While the claims for its currency use are exaggerated, ochre was widely traded, in modern times, by the aboriginals of the Australian coast as well as among the Apache and Mohave Indians of Arizona. Interestingly, in at least one area of the Solomon Islands, ochre is used to paint the strings on which are bound the natives' teeth and shell money.

human being, cannot endow it with value in the eyes of primitive men. Such stones, or fetishes, even when partly shaped by hand, form one of the commonest types of "personal medicine," and possess healing powers which are the sole property of the owner. The celebrated "amazon stones," which are discussed in one of our chapters, seem to have been fetishes of this sort, as well as a convenient and widespread currency.

Feathers, representing their respective birds, are possibly unexcelled in the richness of their associations and imagery. As the wind, the primeval creative breath, the soul, rain, and various individual deities or their companions, they must have entered very early into the select stock of Man's magicoreligious possessions. Being more susceptible to the elements than are stones, teeth and shells, their ancient presence cannot be so easily detected. Yet, feather headdresses may be seen on European rock paintings ten thousand years old, and are known in the Near East even in historical times.

Within metal-working, or "Bronze-Age," cultures, magic, while not dissipated as a vital force, seems, at least, to exercise a less pervasive influence. Accordingly, we find a growing secularization of the desiderata, and, hence, of the currency. For the first time, one observes the use of such items as tools, weapons and cloth as media of exchange. Man still cherished those objects which he believed sustained him, but there seems to have been a growing attachment to physical as opposed to occult relationships. However, for many centuries, even millenia, these two opposing value criteria would operate side by side, as often as not combining in a single medium. Where technology continued to evolve, the original significance of the desideratum was eventually obscured, and its value, when maintained, was done so through custom. We still covet gold and silver, and use them as money, but the association of these metals with solar and lunar deities has long been forgotten.

It is at once intriguing and disappointing to learn that that culture which, in many ways, was the highest in the Americas at the time of the Conquest, possessed no money. One can, of course, understand how a moneyless economy might obtain in a socialist state, or even in a futuristic capitalist one with all-purpose department stores and an unlimited credit system. But how could it operate among the Incas, who were neither socialists nor capitalists, and who had, moreover, the wealth of the Andes at their disposal?* To answer

---

* We have no way of knowing whether this was true also of their predecessors. Excavations among the Chimu, whose own empire was absorbed into that of the Inca, have brought to light small unmarked discs of gold, silver and bronze, perforated for stringing. This fact, together with the existence in pre-Columbian Peru of balance scales identical to European ones, suggests the possibility that these discs, or other convenient metallic forms, may have enjoyed monetary use.

this question, and, indeed, to properly assess Incan economy, we must briefly examine the general subject of archaic politico-economic theory. For the Incan model, however streamlined, was essentially an archaic one.

The basic condition of a pure archaic economy is autocracy. The ruler has inherent proprietory rights over the land and the people, entitling him to the entire produce of the former and labors of the latter. These rights derive from the conviction that he is descended from the particular deity to whom the state belongs, and rules in his (or her) place. Thus, when the worker receives his plot of land, it is not because he is entitled to it. He does not even receive it as a loan (though historians are wont to assert this), but rather as a responsibility. For he must till the whole of it, and any benefit he derives is purely *Dei gratia*.

This simplistic system offers many potential advantages since, barring external pressures, the autocrat has full regulatory powers, and need not contend with the conflicting interests of any internal block. The success or failure of the system depends on his own capabilities, as on those to whom he delegates the responsibilities of administration.

At the top of the Peruvian religio-politico-economic pyramid, inviolable and ostensibly divine like the Egyptian Pharoah, was the lord Inca. He too was descended from the sun, owned everything, and married his sister to maintain the purity of the royal family.

As in Egypt, the Peruvian peasant worked both the "public" and "private" lands, and was conscripted to work on various state projects. The uniqueness of the Incan system, in so far as such a statement is justified, lay in its superior application. However, since the empire, at the time of the Conquest, was less than two centuries old, its very novelty may have been the reason why it had not succumbed to the corruption that gradually undermined Egyptian dynastic rule.

In any case, a dishonest, or self-seeking, Incan official was a real *rara avis,* and received no second chance. Moreover, little distinction was made between dishonesty and ineptitude. If any worker were driven to crime out of actual need, the official responsible for his condition paid the penalty.

The base of the Incan pyramid consisted of ordinary, able-bodied workers. Authority proceeded in decimal divisions so that, at every level of operations, ten men were accountable to one overseer. This continued right up to the provincial governor. Then, four ministers took over, each of whom ruled a quarter of the kingdom, and was responsible only to the lord Inca.

Under the Peruvian system, the worker did not remit a percentage of his own agricultural produce, but paid an equivalent tax by having to work additional lands. These were the lands of the lord Inca and the Inca nobility, the lands of the Sun, which were controlled by the priesthood, and the lands of those who, for reason of infirmity, old age, or absence resulting from conscription, were unable to perform their own work. When he was not engaged in tilling any of the above-mentioned lands, the worker was "free" to attend to that which had been alloted to his own clan.

At any time, however, he was liable to be called away to work on such sundry projects as building a road, mining, or conquering a new territory. Since many projects took years to complete, and some were especially odious, work crews were quickly rotated. Each man's activities were recorded, on knotted strings, with a thoroughness that would do justice to an IBM machine, and no one was obliged to work more, or managed to work less, than the amount stipulated by the State.

It was during his leisure time that the worker became a capitalist. His particular line of work depended on his district, for each had been assigned a speciality and could engage in no other. This rule enabled the Inca planners to maintain a constant equilibrium between the production and consumption of the empire, as well as of its various parts.

Now when the worker was loaded down with his manufactures, what did he do with them? Obviously he couldn't wander from district to district to barter for his needs. In attacking the problem of distribution, the Inca planners fell back up on their two chief resources, ingenuity and skill. What they did was to establish, at centrally located sites, various markets where the people could meet to exchange their goods. Although prices were far from fixed, the production was so closely controlled by demand that the market effectively served as a commodity clearinghouse.

I have so far detailed only the advantages of Incan economy. There were disadvantages also, or rather limitations, for the same ideology that could guarantee to every citizen his shelter, food, clothing, and equal justice before the law, was not prepared to extend its benevolence much further. Thus, while the lord Inca squandered inconceivable sums to entertain himself, or to decorate the walls of his principal buildings, the worker passed his days in a windowless hut. While gold and silver gleamed in the stalls of the great markets, they were available to none but the nobility.* The worker, then, was not even permitted the luxury of greed! But, after all, he had no inherent rights, and, theoretically, his very existence was justified only in so far as he served his emperor.

Aztec political economy was more typically Neolithic. The ruler was still

---

* The ostensible reason was that both metals were sacred, gold being the "sweat of the sun," silver the "tears of the moon."

elected, and whatever supernature he possessed came from his office, as in the case of the Pope. The land belonged to the community, and was divided among the clans. An individual plot was lent to each member at the time he entered upon the responsibilities of marriage. As in Peru, the Aztec paid a tax by working lands other than his own, and by serving in public works. But beyond this, except in relation to his clan, life was not unduly regulated.

No attempt seems to have been made to control production, and the community surplus was regularly borne away by guild merchants who traded what they could in other territories, and returned with items unavailable at home.

Because of the importance of their profession, merchants were exempted from the usual work tax. Another reason for this concession (if we accept some contemporary opinions), is that they also served as spies, furnishing such information about the towns they visited as would be militarily useful to the Aztecs.

No less important than trade to this aggressive people was a wide-reaching system of tribute. Such, of course, entailed war, and plenty of it. New vassals were constantly recruited, and as the multitude of slaves, whose ritual sacrifice was necessary to insure victory, could themselves be obtained only through conquest, the whole, gory process was self-perpetuating.

If the Aztec merchants were deceitful, the tribute collectors were arrogant. That, in any case, was the opinion of the Spanish soldier Bernal Diaz, who encountered some of them at Vera Cruz.[2] They approached the Spaniards "with the utmost assurance and arrogance," and then passed by without speaking a word. "Their cloaks," recalled Diaz even after so many years, "were richly embroidered, and their shining hair was gathered up as though tied on their heads, and each one was smelling the rose that he carried, and each had a crooked staff in his hand. Their Indian servants carried fly-wisks."

At the time of the Conquest, there were hundreds of towns whose tribute regularly swelled the coffers of Montezuma. The Tezozemoc Chronicle[3] records a typical moment in the life of the growing Aztec economy. The year was 1497, and Ahuitzotl, the ruler previous to Montezuma (and the latter's uncle) was in the process of annihilating a federation of coastal tribes. Not surprisingly, this led to a petition by the women and elders of the vanquished, who sued thus for peace:

"Our lords let us speak. We will pay you tribute of all that is produced and yield on these coasts, which will be *chalchihuitl* of all kinds and shades [i.e. jade and various other green stones], other small precious stones named *teoxhuitl* [turquoise] for inlaying in precious objects, and much gold, besides the most exquisite plumage to be found in the whole world, prepared skins of the ocelot, puma and large coyotes, and various kinds of stones streaked with veins of different colors."

We know from Aztec tribute books that many other articles were regularly extorted by the lords of Tenochtitlan. There was, for example, the cotton that made not only heavy armor for the warriors, but the luxurious finery that moved Cortes to remark: "Considering that it was cotton and not silk, there was nothing like it in the whole world, for texture, colors, and handiwork." There was the cacao that Montezuma quaffed from golden cups, and the rubber for the ball games. There were the numerous foodstuffs, and countless other items that would later reappear in the stalls of the great Aztec market.

For the Spaniards, Tenochtitlan, the Aztec city-state, was a place of endless wonders. The looming pyramid temples, with their blood-stained idols "whose size and magnitude no tongue can describe," the gaudy buildings that seemed to float on the waters of the blue Texcoco, the treasures of the royal palace and its zoo and aviary, all left an indelible impression on that literary soldier, Bernal Diaz. Yet, if we judge from the amount of space he devotes to it, Diaz was not less impressed by the Aztec market. Indeed, he tells us that some of the soldiers, who had been in the greatest cities of the world, declared that "so large a market place and so full of people, and so well regulated and arranged, they had never beheld before." Cortes described it in detail,[4] and since it was the chief repository for many of our currencies, the reader may find the quotation to be of interest.

"The city has many squares where markets are held, and trading is carried on. There is one square, twice as large as that of Salamanca, all surrounded by arcades, where there are daily more than sixty thousand souls, buying and selling, and where are found all kinds of merchandise produced in these countries, including food products, jewels of gold and silver, lead, brass, copper, zinc, stone, bones, shells, and feathers. Stones are sold, hewn and unhewn, adobe bricks, and wood, both in the rough and manufactured in various ways. There is a street for game, where they sell every sort of bird, such as chickens, partridges, quails, wild ducks, fly-catchers, widgeons, turtle-doves, pigeons, reed-birds, parrots, owls, eaglets, owlets, falcons, sparrow-hawks and kestrels, and they sell the skins of some of these birds of prey with their feathers, heads, beaks and claws. They sell rabbits, hares, and small dogs which they castrate and raise for the purpose of eating.

"One street is set apart for the sale of herbs, where can be found every sort of root and medicinal herb which grows in the country. There are houses like apothecary shops, where prepared medicines are sold, as well as liquids, ointments, and plasters. They have places like our barber's shops, where they wash and shave their heads. There are houses where they supply food and drink for payment. There are men such as in Castile are called porters, who carry burdens. There is much wood, charcoal, braziers made of earthenware, and mats of diverse kinds for beds, and others, very thin, used as cushions, and for carpeting halls and bedrooms. There are all sorts of vegetables, and especially onions, leeks, garlic, borage, nasturium, water-cresses, sorrel, thistles and artichokes. There are many kinds of fruits, amongst others cherries, and prunes, like the Spanish ones. They sell bees-honey and wax, and honey made of corn stalks, which is as sweet and syrup-like as that of sugar, also honey of a plant called maguey, which is better than most; from these same plants they make sugar and wine, which they also sell.

"They also sell skeins of different kinds of spun cotton, in all colors, so that it seems quite like one of the silk markets of Granada, although it is on a greater scale; also as many different colors for painters as can be found in Spain, and of as excellent hues. They sell deer skins with all the hair tanned on them, and of different colors; much earthenware, exceedingly good, many sorts of pots, large and small, pitchers, large tiles, an infinite variety of vases, all of very singular clay, and most of them glazed and painted. They sell maize, both in the grain and made into bread, which is very superior in its quality to that of the other islands and the mainland; pies of birds, and fish, also much fish, fresh salted, cooked, and raw; eggs of hens and geese and other birds in great quantity, and cakes made of eggs.

"Each kind of merchandise is sold in its respective street, and they do not mix their kinds of merchandise of any species; thus they preserve perfect order. Everything is sold by a kind of measure, and, until now, we have not seen anything sold by weight.

"There is in this square a very large building, like a Court of Justice, where there are always ten or twelve persons, sitting as judges, and delivering their decisions upon all cases which arise in the markets. There are other persons in the same square who go about continually among the people, observing what is sold, and the measures used in selling, and they have been seen to break some which are false."

Notwithstanding the immensity of the picture painted by Cortes, it was still far from complete. After almost a half century, Bernal Diaz recalled, for example, the "Indian slaves both men and women; and I say that they bring as many of them to that great market for sale as the Portuguese bring negroes from Guinea; and they brought them tied to long poles, with collars round their necks. . ." Then there were the "cloths of henequen and ropes and the sandals with which they were shod . . . paper, which, in this country is called *amal,* and reeds scented with liquidambar, and full of tobacco. . ."

Like Cortes, Diaz makes a good try at it, but realizing the futility of his task, he interjects: "Why do I waste so many words in recounting what they sell in that great market?—for I shall never finish if I tell it all in detail."

By comparison to the barbaric splendor of the sun kingdoms, the accomplishments of their northern neighbors seem eminently pale. Search as we may, we nowhere discover Man the city planner, the cunning metallurgist. And yet, even in this Neolithic* wilderness, one does not have to look very far for Man the merchant, nor ferret deeply to discover a number of primitive currencies and long-standing monetary traditions.

Withal, a word of caution should be given concerning the occasional claim for an indigenous American Indian coinage. Columbus, who invented this fiction, was also the first to refute it. He had come to realize that when an aboriginal dangled a golden disc from his nose, he was being no more commercial than a Spaniard wearing golden earrings.

Subsequent commentators have not always been so astute. One writer, for example, speaks of the ancient obsidian coins of Utah, and another, dilating on his remarks, ventures to suggest that the coins are from Sumeria or archaic Egypt. In such a discussion, the fact that coinage was not invented until the seventh century B.C. would seem irrelevent.

Without laboring the point, I would like to say that coinage was wholly unknown to the American Indian, and that attributing artifacts as coins simply because they are round, flat, and inscribed, is contrary to every principle of archeology, economics, and, indeed, responsible journalism.

* Though they worked copper cold for thousands of years, the North American Indians seem never to have learned the art of smelting.

Part I

*MEXICO, AND
CENTRAL AND SOUTH AMERICA*

1. Origins

In the absence of domesticated cattle, the early economic picture of the Americas differs from that of the Old World. Still, there were the agricultural products, and, among these, cotton and cacao, which were not everywhere obtainable, became stores of value, and, in some instances, media of exchange. The other pre-Columbian currencies of Mexico and Central America were luxury items and manufactures. Some, like jade and shells, had doubtless been in use for many centuries,* while others may best be considered as a commercial reflex of the eleventh century technological revolution.**

* The Olmecs, whose own civilization in Mexico was already thriving several centuries B.C., were renowned for their wealth in jade, cacao and plumes, all of which later served the Aztecs as currency.

** During the first millenium A.D., metallurgical knowledge spread from the Andes to centers in Panama and Costa Rica. Thence it trickled northward into Mayadom, a cultural hegemony which extended for some five hundred miles between southern Mexico and Honduras. Unlike the Aztecs and Incas, the Maya neither mined nor refined their own ores, depending rather on trade for a continuous supply of metal. They seem to have produced little in the way of gold, but were prolific manufacturers of small copper articles such as bells and axes. By the eleventh century, metallurgical technique reached the Anahuac Valley, in the Central Mexican plateau. There, in the hands of Mixtec craftsmen, it was transformed into an art that rivalled the best of Peru. Other Andean innovations continued to move north, and thus, at the time of the Conquest, there was not an appreciable difference in quality between the best Peruvian and Mexican handicrafts.

27

The Aztecs, however, had another explanation, and, as usual, it involved Quetzalcoatl. Now Quetzalcoatl, whose name means "the plumed serpent," is the great wind deity of Mexico. He is also, as we might expect from the primeval associations that surround the wind, the god of life and fertility, the creator of Mankind in one of the world cycles, and the inventor of agriculture. Finally, he is the giver of wealth, for such originally derived from the fields of corn, beans and squash. The learned monk Sahagun, quoting from Aztec tradition, thus ascribed to Quetzalcoatl the arts of cutting jade and working silver, the possession of "all the wealth of the world in gold, silver and chalchivites (jade)" together with "a great abundance of cacao trees of different colors," and the building of houses of gold, silver, jade, turquoise and (quetzal) plumes.[5]

It is noteworthy that Quetzalcoatl was never credited with having invented, say, the step pyramid, or contributing anything to the monumental architecture for which Mexico, like Peru, is so justly celebrated. He appears rather as a god of wealth, teaching only those crafts that would enrich the people. In so far as folklore is concerned, he was, without doubt, the father of Aztec currency.

2. Cloth, Feathers and Gold

When Montezuma wished to show his appreciation of Bernal Diaz' courtesy, he could think of no higher compliment than to attribute to the young solder "the qualities of cloth and gold." In English, we say that a person is "pure gold," or has "sterling qualities," and mean the same thing. Numismatically, the Aztec expression serves to underline the importance of cloth and gold, not merely as Mexican currencies, but also as measures of value.

To the Aztec, cotton meant not only warmth, but protection. From it, he made the heavy quilted armor that was adjudged by the Spaniard to be superior to his own. As fate would have it, cotton could not be grown in the Anahuac Valley because of its high elevation. It thus became a principal article of Aztec import trade and tribute.

According to the *Codex Mendoza*[6] one *quachtli,* or large cotton mantle, could purchase a canoe. Thirty of these, we are told, would pay for an ordinary slave, and forty, one who could both sing and dance.

Among the Maya, "small squares of cotton woven fabric called *patalquechtli,*" served as the unit of exchange.[7] Apropos, Prescott[8] relates how Nezhualcoyotl, King of Texcoco, paid an incognito visit to the market place, and hearing the plaints of an impoverished woodcutter and his wife, ordered his officers to give them "a quantity of cloth and a generous supply of cacao."

As early as Olmec times, various plumes had already become an important store of value. Still, their use could not have been too great by comparison to that of the latter days when, thanks to the Peruvian invention of

29

feather weaving, they became the rage of two continents. Among the Aztecs, feathered mantles served as currency, and were so highly valued that a single mantle could purchase one hundred canoes. At such a rate, it is doubtful whether feather goods were possessed by any but the more affluent, or the warriors who required an elaborate headgear in order to overawe the enemy. "Warriors so accoutered," Von Hagen philosophically observed, "die beautifully."

For the nobility, it was desirable also to live beautifully, or at least decoratively. And since, for this purpose, even the great influx of tribute plumes did not suffice, Montezuma caused a royal aviary to be built. Here, according to Bernal Diaz, "there was everything from the Royal Eagle and other small eagles, and other birds of great size, down to tiny birds of many-colored plumage, also the birds from which they take the rich plumage [*i.e.* the quetzal] which they use in their green feather work."

Today, though we have specimens from Peru, only one major example of Mexican feather work, a headdress, survives. The shape resembles a fan, and the beautiful quetzal feathers are bound by successive borders of gold ornamentation and peacock blue and brown featherwork. It is, no doubt, the most beautiful monetary item in the world.

The Maya, though they esteemed a good many plumes, seem only to have used those of the quetzal as money. These must have possessed very great value, for the quetzal, in addition to hiding itself in certain Guatemala highland forests, was sacred to Quetzalcoatl. The only legal way to capture one was to stun it with a clay pellet shot from a blow gun. It was a capital offense to kill the bird.

After their preoccupation with human sacrifice, the Aztecs are most celebrated for their wealth in gold. On numerous occasions, when Cortes and his men were approaching the Aztec city of Tenochtitlan, they were able to procure from the natives various gold artifacts in return for ordinary glass beads. Nevertheless, the motives of these Mexicans were not so simple as they might seem. It would certainly be false to assume that they considered gold a common substance without any particular value. On the contrary, gold served as a medium of exchange throughout the Valley, and was one of the regular tribute items demanded by the Aztecs of their less fortunate neighbors.

Moreover, the Mexicans, with their ubiquitous markets, and highly educated commercial sense, were not likely to be gulled by any old baubles, as were their country cousins in North America. Why then did they agree to such exchanges?

The reason is rather curious, and, not unexpectedly, it involves Quetzalcoatl. This time, however, we are not so much concerned with the deity as with a certain Toltec priest-king, Ce Acatl Topiltzin Quetzalcoatl. According to one version, Topiltzin had sought to establish a more enlightened religion among his people; but, in the end, his attempt to abolish human sacrifice led to a civil war and exile for the King and his loyalists. Afterwards, the remaining Toltecs were themselves driven out of their home in Tula, and some settled in the Anahuac Valley. The history of the Aztecs intertwines with that of the Toltecs on two occasions, the first in Tula, which the former besieged and destroyed, the second in the Anahuac Valley where both tribes later migrated and intermixed. The Aztecs, who were always fond of borrowing other peoples' traditions, perpetuated the story of Topiltzin Quetzalcoatl, the king in exile, who had vowed one day to return. This, it was thought, would take place in the year of his birth, which, according to the Aztec cyclic calendar, occurred once every fifty-two years, and was due again in 1519. As a matter of fact, because of a number of unusual and ominous events (earthquakes, floods, famine, etc.) which were recorded for the years approaching that date, it was widely believed by the Mexicans that the calamity was at hand. Moreover, as Quetzalcoatl (in his aspect as the dawn god) was regarded as white-skinned, and having his abode in the east, and as Quetzalcoatl the god and Topiltzin Quetzalcoatl were generally confused by the Aztecs, one can readily see why the landing of Cortes and his men in 1519, their determination to reach Tenochtitlan, and their willful destruction of sacrificial idols, were all interpreted as the fulfillment of the ancient prophecy.

Montezuma, in great fear, sought to learn what sort of a being Cortes might be, while trying at the same time to curry favor with the Conquistador. Noting the Spaniards' obsession with gold, he wisely ordered his vassals to trade what they had. Indeed, "trade" is scarcely the right word. For if, in those initial days, the Spaniards had refused to make any recompense, they probably would not have been much poorer for it. And this is the true reason for that brief irrational commerce in gold.* Lest any doubts remain, we have two pertinent references in Cortes' letter of October 20, 1520, to King Charles. In one place, Cortes describes how he had demanded gold from a Caltanmi chief as a sign of the latter's vassalage to the Spanish Crown. The chief replied that he would give none unless Montezuma commanded it; and since the order had not yet been given, the former did not part with any. Elsewhere, describing the Spaniards' encampment with their allies, the Tlascalans, Cortes remarks: "... the natives received us very well, and somewhat relieved our

---

* The earlier movements of Grijalba and his men were already known to Montezuma who is said to have expressed great relief at their departure. Even then, the gold that was acquired in these first trades was adjudged by Cuban Governor Diego Velázquez as little in proportion to what he had expected.

great hunger and weariness, although for much of the provision which they gave us they asked payment, and would only accept gold. This we were obliged in our great necessity to give."

The Mexicans were at once relieved and disgusted by the Spaniards' inordinate cupidity. Sahagun, repeating an Aztec account of the first meeting between Cortes' and Montezuma's men, tells how the former were wont to seize upon a gift of gold "like monkeys," and how they "stuffed themselves with it, and starved and lusted for it like pigs."

According to Bernal Diaz, Montezuma kept in his palace a treasure trove of "bars and jewels of gold." Yet, there seem not to have been any restrictions on the public consumption of the metal, and it was exchanged in various forms. Indeed, the first merchants whom Diaz mentions in his description of the great Aztec market were dealers in gold and silver. The former had brought "gold for sale in grains, just as it is taken from the mines. The gold is placed in the thin quills of the geese of the country, white quills, so that the gold can be seen through, and according to the length and thickness of the quills they arranged their accounts with one another."*

Although gold, like everything else, was measured out, Sahagun felt that the skillful merchant knew "the value of gold and silver, according to its weight and fineness, is diligent and solicitous in his duty, and defrauds not in weighing, but rather gives overweight," and this too "in the time of their infidelity."

We know of at least one form, possibly two, in which gold was cast for monetary purposes. Bancroft reviews the matter thus:[9]

"Sahagun says the Mexican king gave to the Merchant soldiers, dispatched on one of their politico-commercial expeditions, sixteen hundred *quauhtli,* or eagles, to trade with. Bustamante, Sahagun's editor, supposes these to have been the copper pieces already mentioned, but Brasseur believes, from the small amount of the copper and the large amount of the rich fabrics purchased with the eagles, that they were of gold. The same authority believes that the golden quoits with which Montezuma paid his losses at gambling also served as money."

I am inclined to agree with Brasseur[10] on both points, especially concerning the eagles of which specimens, in the form of ceremonial labrets, are now known. Besides, since the Aztecs regarded the eagle as their national bird (one having identified to them the site of their home in the Anahuac Valley), the casting of stylized gold eagle ingots was quite in keeping with good mone-

---

* The specimen Quiggen attributes to the Knox collection, in Buffalo, is actually a turkey quill of apparently modern fabrication.

Gold discs, in a variety of sizes, unmarked or with a simple aniconic design, circulated all the way from pre-Columbian Mexico to Peru. Although primarily intended to serve as jewelry, some undoubtedly were used as money. *Courtesy of the Museum of the American Indian, Heye Foundation.*

tary usage. It was tantamount to stamping on the ingots "made and guaranteed by the King of Tenochtitlan".

The so-called "quoits," with which Montezuma paid off Cortes, might more accurately be called "discs," for such is the meaning of *tejulo,* the word used by Diaz in describing the incident. Following the estimate of Diaz, that the *tejulo* was worth some fifty ducats (about $115.), Valentini[11] associated it with the disc a goldsmith is shown holding in the *Codex Mendoza.* In fact, unmarked gold discs, and others with simple aniconic patterns, have been found in a variety of standardized sizes all the way from pre-Columbian Mexico to Peru, and it would seem probable that some, at least, enjoyed monetary use.

Yet, golden discs and golden eagles together comprised but a small part of Montezuma's treasure. This was verified by the Spaniards in the most ecstatic terms, after they surreptitiously broke into the palace storeroom. Cortes, in his second letter to King Charles, describes the wondrous scene:

"Besides their value, these things are so marvellous that for novelty and strangeness they have no price, nor is it likely that any prince in the world possesses such treasures. What I say must appear fabulous to Your Majesty, but the fact is that everything ever created on land and sea of which Montezuma has ever heard was imitated in gold and silver and precious stones, and featherwork, with such perfection that they seemed almost real."

That Cortes was not overstating the case is evident from the reaction of no less an authority than Albrecht Dürer, the celebrated artist and engraver. After examining a gift of Aztec treasure that was being presented to the Spanish king, Dürer wrote in his diary:[12]

"I saw the things which were brought to the King from the New Golden Land; a sun entirely of gold, a whole fathom broad; likewise a moon entirely of silver, just as big; likewise sundry curiosities from their weapons, arms and missiles . . . all of which is fairer to see than marvels. . . .

"These things were all so precious that they were valued at 100,000 gulden. But I have never seen in all my days what so rejoiced my heart as these things. For I saw among them amazing artistic objects and I marvelled over the subtle ingenuity of the men in these distant lands. Indeed I cannot say enough about the things which were there before me."

Today, very little Aztec gold work survives. Almost everything that the Spaniards acquired went into their melting pots, and what Cortes and his men lost in their early flight from Tenochtitlan was never recovered. This later became a source of dispute between Cortes and the Spanish King who suspected his viceroy of double dealing. Whether the Aztecs threw their treasure into Lake Texcoco, as they claimed, or hid it elsewhere, has never been de-

UPPER RIGHT Aztec gold eagle, a standardized form of currency. UPPER LEFT AND BELOW: Jade beads, a valuable currency throughout southern Mexico and Central America. *Courtesy of the Museum of the American Indian, Heye Foundation.*

termined. However, Cortes was apparently telling the truth when he wrote to the King on October 15, 1524: ". . . neither jewels of gold or silver, nor feather work, or any other rich articles are to be obtained as formerly, except little [debased] trinkets of gold and silver, but even these not as in former times."

In the end, Cortes' own officers, most of whom served him in the hope of acquiring great wealth, were forced to settle for tracts of land, together with servants to work them.

3. Jade

Of the various pre-Columbian currencies, none was so highly esteemed as jade. This is confirmed by many sources, one of whom—Bernal Diaz—informs us that jade beads were valued by the Indians "more than emeralds are by us."

Some confusion has resulted from the general equation of jade with the Mexican *chalchihuitl*. The latter was actually a generic term which denoted not only jade, but all kinds of green stones excepting turquoise, which was called *teoxihuitl*. Concerning the different species of *chalchihuitl*, Sahagun had the following to say:

"Precious stones are not found in the beautiful, polished and brilliant condition in which they are sold by venders. They are originally rough, without the appearance of beauty, and are carried from the fields and villages. There are persons who know where precious stones grow because wherever the latter are, they exhale, at dawn, a vapor like delicate smoke. Another sign indicates the place where precious stones are hidden, especially in the case of those called *chalchihuitls*. Wherever these are, the grass which grows above is always green, for the reason that these stones continually send forth a moist exhalation. Wherever this is the stones are to be found in which the chalchihuitls are formed. . . . There is a kind of stone called *quetzal-chalchihuitl* which is named thus because it is like chalchihuitl and is very green. The good stones of this kind are without any spots and are transparent[?] and are

37

very green. There are other stones named *chalchihuitl* which are not transparent and are green mixed with white. This kind is very much used by the chieftains who string them and wear them around their wrists. They constitute a sign that the wearer is a nobleman. It is illicit for vassals to wear them.

"There is another stone belonging to the species of *chalchihuitl,* which is called *tlilaiotic,* and is a mixture of black and green.

"Besides the above mentioned stones there are other jasper stones of many kinds and colors. . . . Some of these are white as well as green and therefore called *iztachalchihuitl.* Others have green veins with light blue or other colors mixed with the white."

Some writers have equated Sahagun's *quetzal-chalchihuitl* with the American species of jade, and while this may be correct, it does not explain why the friar described the stone as transparent, or said it was "like *chalchihuitl.*" I am inclined to believe that the word *chalchihuitl* referred, in general usage, to all green stones, but in specific usage was restricted to jade alone. This would explain why the other green stones were often referred to as simply *chalchihuitls,* though, as Sahagun illustrates, they could be differentiated according to the species.

It appears that while all of the *chalchihuitls* were considered precious, only the "true" *chalchihuitl* served as currency. The most specific indication of its value was given by Montezuma, who (according to Bernal Diaz) told Cortes: "I will also give you some very valuable stones which you will send to him [King Charles] in my name; they are *chalchivites** and are not to be given to any one else but only to him, your great Prince. Each stone is worth two loads of gold."

In their desperate flight from Tenochtitlan (culminating their first military encounter with the Aztecs), the Spaniards had to forsake a vast amount of gold given to Cortes by Montezuma. Perhaps with a sense of irony, Cortes allowed any man to keep what valuables he could take with him, and a good many lost their lives because of greed. Bernal Diaz, with better sense, took only "some small boxes that were there . . . and four chalchivites . . . and I quickly placed them in my bosom under my armour, and, later on, the price of them served me well in healing my wounds and getting me food."

So the beautiful jade beads that were intended for none but King Charles ended up in part rehabilitating a common foot soldier. For this small irony, or, if you will, kindness of fate, Bernal Diaz reciprocated in his old age by penning his marvellously descriptive epic on the siege of Mexico.

---

* Diaz was never able to master the Nahuatl word *chalchihuitl,* and always substituted the Spanish corruption "chalchivite."

I have earlier mentioned the Mexican use of jade in burials. Bishop Landa, who closely observed Maya customs in order to more effectively suppress them, has left us the following description:

"Once dead, they put them in a shroud, filling their mouths with ground maize, which is their food and drink which they call *Koyem,* and with it they placed some of the stones which they use for money, so that they should not be without something to eat in the other life."

From Landa's description, it appears that the original significance of the ritual had become somewhat obscured among the Maya by the growing commercial value of jade. An identical obscuration occurred in China, and an even more complete one in Greece, where a coin was placed in the mouth of the corpse to provide his fare to the next world.*

The Aztecs, like the Egyptians, retained the ritual in its purer, esoteric form. The latter placed on the chest of the deceased a large scarab cut from green stone, and engraved with instructions for the protection of his heart. The same idea seems to have been intended by the Aztecs, of whom Sahagun writes:

"They also say that when a chief or noble died they placed a green stone (chalchivite) into his mouth as he was dying. In the mouth of a dying person of the lower classes they did not insert such a precious stone, but one of little value which is called *texoxoctli* or knife stone [flint or obsidian?] which, they said, represented the heart of the deceased."

It might seem, from the use of inferior stones for the same purpose, that the ritual was not taken too seriously. This, however, would be a misinterpretation. The answer lies rather in the Aztec's belief that the after world was socially stratified like the one in which he presently lived. An individual's destination was determined not by the quality of his terrestrial days, but by his class. The affluent went to realms where they could live in the manner to which they were accustomed; and the poor proles did likewise! This must have been why the latter could get along with an inferior stone. One does not require a golden key to unlock a leaden door.

In varying degrees, all green stones seem to have been considered precious by the Aztecs. In fact, due to the association of the quetzal bird with Quetzalcoatl (who, despite Topiltzin Quetzalcoatl, was still revered by the Aztecs), green was the royal color. The preeminence of jade may have been explained by the myth that Quetzalcoatl was born through a miraculous conception after

---

* In Greek mythology this practice was associated with Charon, the aged and dirty ferryman. The concept apparently reached Greece in later times as Charon is not mentioned by any of the early Greek poets.

his mother swallowed a piece of that mineral. This story, incidentally, provides one more connection between jade and the creative life force.

In the more than four centuries that have passed since the Spanish Conquest, the White Man has proven decidedly inferior to the Indian in locating jade. For all his efforts, the former can boast no more than a handful of inferior deposits. Yet, at one time there were dozens of Mexican tribes whose offerings of jade beads regularly swelled the coffers of Tenochtitlan.

4. Other Early Mexican and Central American Currencies

At least one sort of shell bead seems to have enjoyed currency status among the Maya, for Compocolche, in his *Relacion*,[13] tells us that an idol was presented with "some green stones which they call *tun* and others which they call *kan* which are red, and these red ones are of value and precious because with them they buy that for which they have need." That this red bead was, in fact, wrought from shell is indicated by both Landa and Cogolludo, the latter of whom,[14] specifically mentions "money which they used . . . some red shells which they import and which they string together like the beads of a rosary." A similar report is contained in the *Relacion* of Gaspar Antonio Chi.[15]

It is a curious fact that silver, though considered precious and sold as a commodity, was never used by the early Mexicans as money. And this seems the more perplexing when we consider that both copper and tin, in certain forms, passed as currency.

Cogolludo, writing of the Maya, states: "The money which they used was copper bells of different sizes which had a value according to their size." A good many of these bells have been recovered from the Cenote of Sacrifice.*

Einzig, on the basis of a fictional reference, cites copper hatchets as an Aztec currency.[16] It is, however, true that these hatchets, or rather axes, served as favored barter items throughout Mexico.

* A renowned sacrificial well which was located at Chichen Itza, the center of Toltec-Maya culture. It attracted Indians from as far away as Colombia, and was the repository of innumerable valuables, including jade. Into its yawning gulfs, an occasional slave was also discharged by his over-zealous master.

41

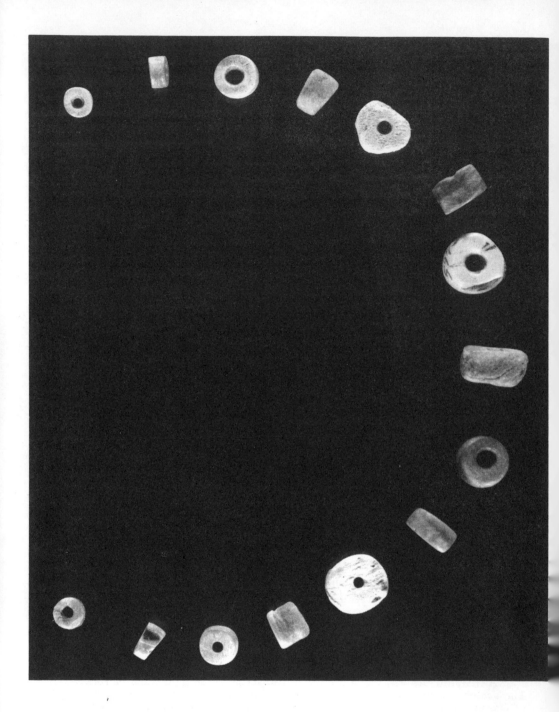

Kan, or red spondylus shell discs, a currency of the Maya. These specimens were dredged from the celebrated sacrificial well at Chichen Itza. *Courtesy of the Peabody Museum, Harvard University.*

Copper bells, a currency of the Maya. *Courtesy of the Museum of the American Indian, Heye Foundation.*

Friar Juan de Torquemada, writing about 1610,[17] refers to "certain copper moneys, almost similar in form to the Greek tau. These were thin planchets, some thinner than others, measuring three or four fingerbreadths and containing much gold."

Torquemada's error with respect to the gold content of the planchets would indicate that they bore a beautiful polish when new. One is reminded of the gaff that Cortes' soldiers made on one occasion when trading with Indians from Coatzacoalcos and neighboring towns. Asked to fetch gold for barter, the natives brought also some highly polished copper axes with painted wooden handles. The Spaniards, believing that the axes contained low-grade gold, eagerly bartered for them, and in three days accumulated a hoard of more than six hundred pieces. The "treasure" was then dispatched by ship to Cuba, where the men unveiled it before the Governor. "When the six hundred axes which we thought were low grade gold were brought out," Bernal Diaz recalls, "they were all rusty like copper which they proved to be, and there was a good laugh at us, and they made great fun of our trading."

Diaz' experience would explain why the copper "T's" referred to by Torquemada were frequently rejected when not in new condition. That this was, in fact, the practice is shown by a letter which Pradeau discovered in the archives at Seville.[18] Written in October, 1548, it also provides the earliest known reference to the currency. The letter, and the accompanying drawing, were sent by Francisco Lopez Tenorio, a Oaxaca resident, to the President of the Council of Indies. According to Pradeau's translation, it reads:

"This is the form of copper coins that were in use in New Spain. The value placed and at which these were commonly accepted was of four such pieces, if new, for five Spanish reales. If worn, many refused to accept them, and then they were sold to be melted at ten pieces for one Spanish real.

"In this and neighboring provinces, the natives use these metallic pieces in great quantities, and with their circulation both Spaniards and aborigines suffer considerable mulcting. This can be remedied if the natives are restrained from manufacturing them, and the medium of exchange shall then be what your Excellency has ordered minted, to circulate in New Spain."

Pradeau devotes several paragraphs to a discussion of the possible uses of the T-shaped coppers, concluding that they "were and are pottery instruments." I confess that, with the same evidence before me, I cannot see in their form anything but a conventionalized axe or hoe blade.*

---

* This parallels, to some extent, the transition in China where the hoe and knife first became favored barter items, and, finally, token currencies, circulating in a degenerate form, as a mere symbol of the original tools and their value.

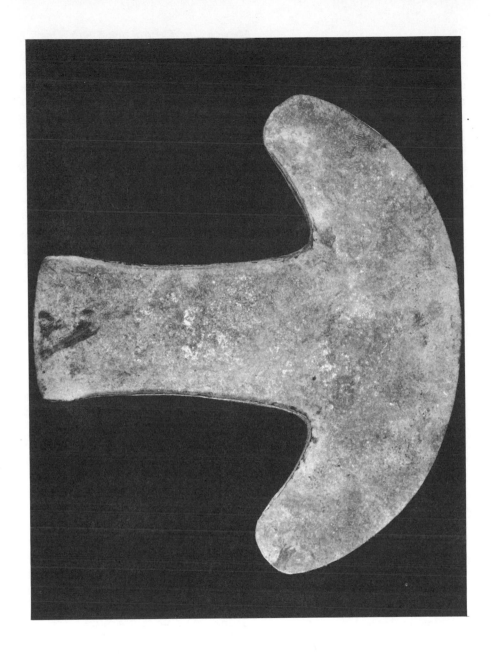

Stylized copper model of axe or hoe blade. This unusual currency circulated in Oaxaca in early post-Columbian times. Its value depended largely on its being in a bright uncirculated condition. *Courtesy of the Chase Manhattan Bank Money Museum.*

Quiggen, following Sir William Ridgeway, favors the former designation, and, indeed, the Aztec glyph for an axe (which is shown on the plate for comparison) shows considerable resemblance to our copper "T's". On the other hand, Dupaix[20] adverts to an ancient picture in Mitla "which represented Saint Isidro, the patron of the laborers . . . holding in his right hand a pole armed with the problematic blade." Both Dupaix and Valentini concluded from this that the "T's" were originally an agricultural tool. So the question remains an open one.

In his letter to King Charles on October 15, 1524, Cortes mentions the use of a tin currency among the natives of certain provinces. He had put his artillery master to work making two medium-sized cannon, and, as tin was also required for these, he procured what he could from natives who had tin plates or other vessels, "but dear or cheap, very little could be found." And so, he tells us: "I then instituted enquiries in every direction for this metal, and it pleased our Lord (who ever protects us, and provides speedily for our wants), that among the natives of a province called Tachco I should meet with little pieces of it resembling very small coins; and continuing my researches, I found it was used as money both in that province and others."

Einzig, following Prescott's lead, confuses the above with Torquemada's reference to the copper axe, money; he thus wrongly concludes that the Mexicans used T-shaped pieces of tin as currency. The actual shape of the Tacho money is nowhere given, and Cortes' reference to "coins" is not instructive. However, a single tin astrological amulet, or disc, a couple of inches in diameter, has been excavated from the sacrificial well at Chichen Itza, and it does not seem impossible that such pieces, like their gold counterparts, enjoyed a currency use.

By far the most common currency of Pre-Columbian America was the cacao bean. In his second letter to the king, Cortes describes it as "a fruit somewhat like almond. . . . This fruit they sell ground, and it is so valued that it is used instead of money all over the country, in the market places and elsewhere."

Merida, in his *Relacion,*[21] writes of the Maya: "They use a great quantity of cacao which is brought from the province of Tabasco and from Honduras, because of it they make their beverages in which they take great delight and consume in this way all or most of what they are able to hoard up from their work and gains and it serves them as money."

Except during the period from January 28, 1527 to October 24, 1536, the beans were always reckoned by count, and sacks containing three *xiquipilli* (24,000 beans) were used to facilitate reckoning. In Nicaragua, a rabbit could be purchased with ten beans, and a slave for one hundred "more or less, according to his condition and the agreement between the seller and buyer."

"Oh blessed money," observed Petrus Martyr with befitting charity;[22] "Oh blessed money which not only gives to the human race a useful and delightful drink, but also prevents its possessors from yielding to infernal avarice, for it cannot be piled up, or hoarded for a long time."

As it turned out, the blessing was a mixed one, for not all possessors of the beans were free from avarice. There was, for example, the case of a native who carefully removed the kernel from each one, and then substituted dirt to compensate for the loss in weight. This led the Spaniards to engage native counterfeit detectors who, by a deft squeeze, could segregate the altered beans from unaltered ones.

5. The Mysterious Money of the Amazons and Other Carib and Arawak Currencies

After the discovery of Tenochtitlan and Cuzco, it required only a whisper of some new source of native wealth to outfit another Spanish expedition. A classic example is the search for the "gilded man."

It appears that, in early times, the king of the Chibcha Indians, who dwelt in the Andean region of Colombia, annually performed a great sacrifice at Lake Guatavita. On the day of the ritual, he would smear his body with an adhesive substance and roll in gold dust. Thus gilded and resplendent, the king, with his retinue and a great quantity of treasure, set out for the sacred lake. When, with due éclat, the party arrived, they boarded the royal barge, and paddled to a place where the water was especially deep. The king then offered a prayer and divested himself, one by one, of the valuables. Finally, he himself plunged into the water and washed the gold from his body. This sacrifice was held annually until about 1480, when Guadavita was conquered by Nemequene.

By 1535, when the Spaniards first heard the story, it had already aged into a legend in which the "gilded man" was accompanied by Manoa, an entire city of gold. Manoa, or, as the Spaniards called it—El Dorado—became a popular obsession, and natives threatened with torture if they failed to reveal its whereabouts, regaled their conquerers with many a fanciful tale.

As time passed, adventurers from other nations began to arrive. Sir Walter Ralegh, like Berrio before him, travelled the Orinoco, and, hearing exaggerated reports about the Caribs, concluded that Manoa lay somewhere

48

in Guiana. Not very long before, the Caribs had migrated from Parana and Paraguay. Being, at once, more advanced and fiercer than the indigines, they quickly overran the whole of the Brazilian littoral, as well as the Orinoco provinces, and finally took the Antilles. Awed by Carib exploits, inferior tribes were inclined to exaggerate when describing them, especially to the over-credulous Europeans.

Though it may have been the cause of it all, the Manoa myth was not the only one to keep adventurers scurrying, for three centuries, through the Guianese jungles. Another involved the Amazons. According to Arawak folklore, there once had lived a Kaieri (Trinidad*) chief named Arawanili who was greatly favored by the village women, and who finally cajoled them, one and all, to leave their families and accompany him to Matinino.** For reasons I will later mention, Arawanili subsequently left the island of Matinino which henceforth was populated entirely by women.

Now the legend of an entire race of women was nothing new to the Europeans. Their own Greek mythology could boast one—that of the Amazons—who dwelt in the Caucasus, and at different times invaded Lycia, Phrygia, and Attica. The Spaniards with their romantic predilections, had no difficulty in equating the two legends, especially as they had frequently encountered women warriors of unusual strength, courage and skill. These Carib women (for such were the best of them), enjoyed a reputation equal to that of their redoubtable husbands, and were fully up to repulsing an attack made during the latters' absence. Yet, for all their skirmishes with the "Amazons," the Spaniards seem to have had no more luck in finding Matinino than they had Manoa.

Schomburgk,[23] the most persistent of a long line of explorers seeking Matinino, observed that the natives invariably located the city just beyond their own familiar horizons. On one such adventure, an Arawak chief related how his brother, then deceased, had visited the Amazons, and received from them a certain green stone as a present. The women were said to work their own fields, and be skillful with the bow and blowpipe. They permitted men to visit them but once a year, and slew all male children. Schomburgk adds with a sigh:

"The old chief had heard this from his brother, but none of the Indians whom I interviewed concerning these fabled women had seen them themselves. This had always been the luck of their grandfather, father, or some relative or other who was not now alive or present. So again, at the source

---

* The earlier home of the Arawaks.
** A fabled island which has sometimes been confused with Martinique.

ABOVE: "Amazon stone," shaped as an animal's head. Sometimes these green stones were made into a cylinder shape, with the animal or fish design incised in low relief. *Courtesy of the Museum of the American Indian, Heye Foundation.* BELOW: A Lengua youth wearing a string of snail-shell disc currency. From an old photograph by W. B. Grubb.

of the Corentyn, where, on account of its being hitherto unknown, a last place of refuge had been found for them, my brother learnt nothing more definite, nor did he discover the Amazons themselves."

As a result of such cross-checking, Schomburgk finally concluded that Matinino did not, in fact, exist. Yet, this only exchanged one snag for another. For, if, indeed, the Amazons didn't exist, how was one to explain the so-called "Amazon stones" which, by all native accounts, were the currency of Matinino?

Sir Walter Ralegh, whose obsession with Guiana finally cost him his royal head, mentions the stones as early as 1618:[24]

"These *Amazones* have likewise great store of these plates of gold, which they recover by exchange for a kinde of green stone, which the Spanish call *Piedras Hijadas,* and we use for spleene stones, and for the disease [sic] of the stone we also esteeme them: of these I saw divers in Guiana, and commonly every king or Casique hath one, which their wives for the most part weare, and they esteeme them as great jewels."

Schomburgk, writing of the stones two-and-a-half centuries later, says:

"Extremely remarkable things at all events are the green Amazon-stones (Lapis nephritious), the *Piedras hijadas* of the Spaniards about which all Indian accounts agree that they come from the Amazons. Alexander Von Humboldt found these stones among the Indians of the Rio Negro where they are carried on the neck as amulets for protection against fever, and bites of poisonous snakes; Von Martius saw them on the Rio Negro among the residents at Sylves, while I came across them in Georgetown. It was through the Caribs along the Guiana coast that these stones were brought into Georgetown where they are known as *Macuaba* or Calicot stones. On the Orinoco they are called *Macagua,* apparently the same term as the former. Formerly, the Caribs brought them to the capital in considerable quantities, but very rarely nowadays. I only once had the opportunity of seeing a specimen which was in the possession of a merchant there. It corresponds accurately enough not only in shape but also in color with the description given by Alexander van Humboldt. From what the people told me, these stones were formerly brought to town in the shape of fish and other animals, as well as with figures carved on their surfaces. According to Barrere, the Caribs treasured them more than gold; such a one was the price of a slave."

Schomburgk, hearing a report of similar stones in Mexico, tentatively assigned their origin to that country. I am unable to substantiate this claim, and very much doubt the conclusion drawn from it, especially as jade is also found in Northeastern Brazil. Besides, the only Amazon stones I have been able to locate are cut not from true jade, but from the softer serpentine. I thus think it not unlikely that they were made and originally circulated by tribes that succumbed to Carib invasions. This, at least, would explain the later scarcity of the stones, and the obscurity surrounding their origin.

By the mid-nineteenth century, Amazon stones were a vanishing currency, and the jade and crystal beads of the Carib and Arawak tribes circulated in their place. Among the continental Arawaks, jade and crystal beads enjoyed great sentimental as well as monetary value. The origin of the latter was associated with Arawanili, the philandering Kaieri chief of whom we have already heard. It seems that during his sojourn on Matinino, Arawanili's excesses resulted, not inexplicably, in a certain disease, to cure which he left the island for another called Guanin. It was on the shore of the latter that the chief was healed by a sea nymph, and subsequently given crystal beads she had fetched from the ocean's floor.

According to Lovin,[25] the upper-class Arawaks used to wear strings of the currency beads, removing the required number when making a purchase. The beads were not individually owned, but considered as part of the family property.

The beads were also used by the Tainos, or Arawaks of the Greater Antilles, but were so scarce that they were mainly owned by Cacique families, and reserved for use as gifts of honor. Regarding the Igneris, or Arawaks of the Lesser Antilles, Lovin says: "No wares go so far as semi-precious stones and the shells of molluscs in trade with tribes living in the remote regions. . . ." Nevertheless, the stones and shells are understood to have served more as favorite barter items than as actual currency.

6. Recent Currencies of Central America

After the Conquest, a good deal of the remaining native Mexican currency was exacted by the Church in penalties for recidivism. According to Bishop Landa, the total fines at one time imposed on the Maya for idol worship included one hundred and twenty-five thousand cacao beans, and numerous jade beads, red shell beads and copper bells. All of these had been confiscated on the ground that they were used in heathen offerings, and were thus sinful to possess.

Yet, no amount of confiscation could affect the cacao bean. In remote areas, it is known to have circulated as currency even within the present century, and, as late as 1940, was still being used in ceremonial payments among the Chorti Indians of Guatemala.

"They are still used in formal gift-making," Wisdom observed,[26] "as between the mother of a new born child and the *padrino* in Quetzaltepeque *municipio;* the cacao is said to be a gift rather than a payment, but its present day ceremonial use is probably a vestige of its wider use as money in the past."

The Chorti also blended the old with the new in making ceremonial coins. Discs called "pesos" were fashioned out of copal gum, and burnt as an offering in the *incensario.*

Another actual currency used by the tribe was shelled maize. The unit was a gourdful, which weighed about one pound. Being the agricultural staple, it was readily accepted by all but a few of the wealthier Indians who possessed a large surplus of their own.

Among the Maya living at Chan Kom, about one fifth of the small local purchases were made with maize. Moreover, as Redfield notes:[27]

"The amount of [coined] money in circulation depends on the time of year and the value of maize; just after the annual harvest has been sold there is more; on the other hand, if people have withheld their surplus maize from the market for a better price, most purchases must be made with eggs, maize or hens."

By the mid-nineteenth century, eggs were already competing with cacao for use as small change. The two commodities did not circulate concurrently, but as popular alternatives in making change for the cuartillo ($3\frac{1}{8}$¢).[28] The exact purchasing power of the eggs varied with their value in the town market. During the period of Redfield's observation (1934), they passed at four centavos each. Travelling merchants were paid chiefly in poultry.

Another alternative to minor coinage was noted by journalist George Kendall, while passing through Queretaro, Mexico, in 1842.[29] Having purchased a half dozen oranges and some sweet limes, he was given, as change for a dollar, sixty-four cakes of soap tied together in a handkerchief. As it turned out, all of the towns in the vicinity issued these cakes as a legal tender, fixing their value at eight to the real (12¢). Moreover:

"Each cake is stamped with the name of the town where it is issued and also with the name of the person who is authorized by law to manufacture it as a circulating medium. Yet, Celaya soap—for it also circulated in that city—will not pass at Queretaro. The reason I cannot divine, as the size and intrinsic value appear to be the same. The municipal authorities of either town appear to have made no provision for equalizing the exchanges between the two pieces, and there are no brokers' offices for the buying and selling of uncurrent soap in Mexico. Many of the cakes in circulation were partially worn, and showed evidence indisputable of an acquaintance with the washtub; but all were current so long as the stamp was visible."

Few primitive currencies come quite so close to disqualifying themselves from that category. Stamped in each case by the issuing authority, how does this Mexican soap currency differ, say, from the velvet notes or porcelain coins of inflationary Germany? One answer is that the material of the German currency was selected as an emergency substitute, and not for any intrinsic worth. Soap, on the other hand, was a vital necessity, and its value derived from its market price.

This, however, opens the way to a second argument, namely that, in the early nineteenth century, gold and silver coins were likewise valued according to their bullion price, leaving the owner the option of melting them down. The counterargument is that whether as coin or bullion, gold and silver constituted money and not merely a commodity. The Mexican soap had no currency status unless cast in a particular form, and not a currency form either, but that which it traditionally bore as a commodity.

Coconuts apparently still circulate as money in Panama, where U.S. currency is also legal tender. A generation ago, the value of one coconut, among the San Blas Indians, was five cents.

7. Other Currencies of South America

The ethno-numismatist must forever be on guard against the encroachment of barter items. Not only must he contend with occasional ambiguities in his source material, but also (and this is by far the more challenging) with his own desire to collect as many citations as possible.

Discrimination is especially important when one approaches the hinterlands, where tribal specialities and regional trade give rise to innumerable favorite barter items. A good many examples are provided by William Smyth, who, during the early nineteenth century, journeyed for hundreds of miles across the Andes and down the Amazon.[30] At Tocache, Smyth was able to obtain a "fine turkey" for five strings of glass beads which, he tells us, had a fixed local value. Now if this incident had been repeated out of context, one might infer from it that the beads (although of European manufacture) served as a native currency. However, a responsible writer would have to add that needles, knives, handkerchiefs, and a certain skin salve were all equally useful at Tocache in obtaining one's necessaries.

Even the prevalence of one particular commodity does not imply a monetary system unless that commodity is always presentable at a given value. Thus, while axes were used for payment at the port of Sarayacu, and sarsaparilla among the Tunautins, Smyth gives no evidence that either served as more than favorite barter items.

In the same category are the beads, guns, arrows and chickens that Einzig erroneously cites as Brazilian currencies.

Still, the picture is not entirely bleak. Smyth himself provides a few examples of primitive money, beginning with the use of coca in Peru.

"If coca did not exist," wrote Cieza de Leon in 1550, "neither would Peru,"[31] — an exaggeration, no doubt, but admissible when we consider that the leaves are found among even ancient grave goods, and were valued by the Incas more highly than were gold and gems. The "divine" leaves were chewed (and sometimes swallowed) for their narcotic properties. They are said to have wrought such diverse benefits as the courrier's stamina and a soothsayer's dreams.

When the Incan empire was overthrown, coca became for the first time available to the ordinary Indian. The concession, however, was not a boon. With its widespread appeal (its deleterious effects then being unknown), coca provided a great incentive to Spanish exploitation. Few Indians could afford to be independent farmers, and the rest were forced to toil for Spanish entrepreneurs, who greatly enriched themselves through the trade. Church tithes and state taxes were collected in coca, and, as of 1604, the learned Jesuit José de Acosta unequivocally called the leaves a currency.[32]

Such was the situation that Smyth encountered at Panao, in the interior of Peru. Even at this date, a laborer received only two rials (one shilling) a day, plus food. How poorly he himself fared while cultivating a currency for his overlord is illustrated by the following quotation:

"With the coca they pay their contribution to the State and the dues to the clergy; the former is three dollars annually for each person between the ages of twenty and sixty. The tenth, called the diezmo, and formerly paid to the church is now received by the government: the church gets a mere trifle, called the premisia. The fees established by law for christening, marriages and interment are, two dollars for the first, twenty-eight dollars or more for the second, and thirty-five for the last. Those of the poor who are unable to pay can neither be christened, married or buried; and it sometimes happens that a body is left unburied until corruption obliges the people to throw it into a ditch and cover it up."

At Tarapoto, in Brazil, Smyth noted the use of a rather unusual commodity currency.

". . . Cotton, gums, resin, and white wax are the principal products of their woods: the latter is formed into round cakes weighing about a pound each, and these are considered the currency of the place, each cake being considered as equivalent to a dollar."

The most widely used commodity money he encountered was a coarse cotton cloth called *tucuya*. It was the special product of the forty or so natives of Juana del Rio, and circulated along the greater part of the Marañon river.

Its great demand was due to the fact that the cloth served to make not only garments, but the sacks required to pack coca.

In nearby Archidona, Ecuador, a similar currency was reported as late as 1923. "In Quito," relates explorer F. W. Up de Graff,[33] they told me that the only unit of exchange that would be of any use to me in Archidona was that particular class of material, which was especially woven in that capital." Up de Graff equipped himself with three bales, from which he later paid two yards each to his porters, and ten yards to his canoemen. "It was a coarse fabric," he confirms, "but a favorite among the Indians."

Accosta mentions the currency use of cloth in connection with Santa Cruz de la Sierra, in Bolivia, but unfortunately provides no details.

Shell disc currency, while not generally associated with the southern continent, is reliably reported among the Lengua, a nomadic Paraguayan tribe.[34] Using an ordinary knife and a snail shell, the Indian fashioned button-sized discs which he then pierced and polished. Throughout the operation, he sat cross-legged on the ground, the heel of his foot serving as a work table. The currency unit, which was a string of beads six yards long, could purchase one sheep. Both men and women wore the strings, which had to be wound a good many times around the body.

Salt was a favorite barter item from Mexico southward, and, at times, has served as a currency among the Indians of Otavalo Valley, in Imabura Province, Ecuador. "Salt is rare in the Andes," wrote John Collier as late as 1949.[35] "It is traded from great distances and is so valuable that it often serves as a medium of exchange."

Cattle, while not indigenous to South America, proliferated rapidly after the Conquest, and, in many backward regions of Colombia, Venezuela and Brazil, became a measure of value, if not a currency. Since commerce almost everywhere outstripped the supply of coins, various other commodity currencies were also adopted.

On February 15, 1712, cloves, coca, sugar and tobacco were officially declared the currency of Brazil, and used to pay the salaries of troops. The historian Felisbello Freire[36] further tells us that "one could find in the captaincies of the North a continuous complaint against the withdrawal of cotton as it was money and was always prohibited from being taken out of the country."

A similar situation prevailed in Argentina. Prior to the seventeenth century, goods were generally bartered at fixed values according to the Spanish currency reckoning. But in Cordoba, as early as 1574, the cabildo decreed that goats and horseshoes should pass as currency.[37] Subsequently, wool, tallow, rams and ewes were added to the roster of commodity currencies. Wedges of iron circulated briefly, but had to be demonetized because of fluctuations in the value of the metal.

Acosta, writing of Paraguay, mentions the use of "stamps of yron for coins." These may have been similar to the wedges just referred to. During the seventeenth century, the Paraguayan government adopted yerba maté and tobacco as currencies. Twenty-five pounds of maté had the purchasing power of two pesos, while tobacco was valued at twice this amount.

In Tierra del Fuego, no currency seems to have been required until the end of the nineteenth century when the otter trade developed. Then, to meet the needs of traders, the cheapest variety of antwerp gin was made current.[38]

The English, in the small measure that they penetrated South America, succumbed to the general pattern of monetary confusion. In Honduras, for example, logwood became the official currency. Chalmers relates:[39]

"The first article of the popular Convention of the 9th April 1765 (with which law began in British Honduras) provides that 'whosoever shall be found guilty of profane cursing and swearing shall . . . forfeit and pay for every such offence the sum of 2s. 6d., Jamaica currency, or the same value in merchantable unchipped logwood."

The liberal value placed by the authorities on their staple discouraged the importation of English coins, "leaving the early currency of the Bay on a purely Mahogany basis." Thus, on May 15, 1766, the legislature at Belize (the chief town of Honduras) decreed "that all Debts contracted in the Bay of Honduras shall be payable in Logwood unless there shall be a special Agreement made between the parties writing to the contrary."

Logwood remained a legal tender in Honduras until June, 1784, when it was resolved that "all wood under 15 inches shall be deemed unmerchantable, and not admitted in payment for debts; That the established price of logwood shall be 6.1 per ton for chipped and 4.1 per ton for unchipped logwood." All previous debts that had been contracted in logwood were now made payable in Jamaica currency "at the established price which may prevail at the time that such payment is made."

Chalmers also records that during the 1840's the situation in British Guiana grew so chaotic that traders resorted to the use of empty bottles and sugar cane as currency.

8. The Lesser Antilles

Because of a comparatively poor mineral wealth, and the extreme ferocity of the Carib inhabitants, the smaller islands of the Indies were left to such late comers as the English and the Dutch. Chalmers has ably described the economic situation under the former, and I can do no more than summarize his findings.

In Barbados, cotton and tobacco were the earliest staples of the island, and, from about 1631 to 1640, served as the principal currencies. Thereafter, they were supplanted by muscovado, or unrefined sugar, which continued to circulate as a medium of exchange until about 1715.

Thus, we find in an "act concerning morning and evening prayer in families" (*ca.* 1645): "Whosoever shall swear or curse, if a master or freeman, he shall forfeit for every such offense four pounds of sugar; if a servant, two pounds of sugar."

At its original valuation, one hundred pounds of sugar equalled ten shillings. However, on September 16, 1667, according to the records of Lord William Willoughby, the assembly 'raised their coin' [*i.e.* muscovado] so that one hundred pounds would equal sixteen shillings. During 1690-92, sugar was revalued at twelve shillings and sixpence, the standard then prevailing elsewhere in the British West Indies.

The currency situation in the Leeward Islands broadly paralleled that of Barbados. At first, tobacco prevailed both as a staple and currency. Chalmers quotes a penal act, the Montserrat Act of 1668, which penalized "one thousand pounds of good marchantable tobacco in Role" any person guilty of "unlawful gaming, immoderate and uncivil drink . . . or any other prophane and illicious Labours of the Week-days, as digging, houghing, baking, crab-bing, and such like indecent Actions."

From 1672 until the end of the century, sugar served as the principal currency. At the same time, tobacco, cotton, wool and indigo enjoyed a limited monetary use and may, perhaps, be considered quasi-currencies.

In Bermuda, tobacco continued as the chief currency until 1684, after which it was gradually supplanted by specie.

Part II

NORTH AMERICA

9. California

Much has been written concerning the preoccupation of the Pacific Coast Indians with wealth and status. Such a preoccupation may, under different conditions, beget violence, sublimate it, or, as generally happens, do both. In the balance, its effect on coastal life seems to have been salubrious, for warfare and violence remained somewhat below average. Conversely, as one might expect, monetary traditions were highly developed.

In southern and central California, the monetary system was analagous to our own bi-metallism. Silver was represented by white clam or snail shell discs, gold by the more valuable golden-orange magnesite cylinder beads. Both, it should be stated at the outset, were in use in pre-contact times. The chief "minters," or purveyors, of the currency were the Chumash and Pomo tribes, and it was through their diligence that Indians in the remoter areas were kept well supplied.

In 1792, the shell discs were noted by José Longinos Martinez, the first trained observer to visit lower California. Martinez, describing the Chumash Indians, of the district around the Santa Barbara Channel, wrote:[40]

"In their bargaining they use, as we use weights, their *poncos* of strings of beads. This word *ponco* is used for a certain measure of these strings, two turns from the wrist to the extended middle finger. The value of the *ponco* depends on the esteem in which the beads are held, according to the difference in fineness and the colors that are common among them, ours being held in higher regard. The value depends upon the greater or smaller extent to which the beads have been circulated, the new value depending upon their abundance. The value which should be placed upon our beads is always

65

estimated with respect to their own, and in everything they keep as much order as the most careful man who has accumulated some money.

"They make their beads out of a species of small sea snail (caracolito), which they break into pieces, shaping them in the form of lentils, then drilling them with our needles and stringing them. After the strings have been made, they rub them down until they bring them to a degree of fineness, for in their conception they have more value so. These strings of beads, and ours, are used by the men to adorn their heads, and for collars which they weave with beads of different designs, like a rope belt, etc. They all make a show of their wealth, which they always wear in sight on their heads, whence it is taken for gambling and trafficking."

Another reference to the Chumash beads appears in the *California Farmer* of June 1, 1860. The writer describes the currency as "supposed to have been manufactured for the most part on Santa Rosa Island [Santa Barbara Channel]," and adds:

"The worth of a rial was put on a string which passed twice and a half round the hand, i.e. from end of middle finger to wrist. Eight of these strings passed for the value of a silver dollar." Each string was one yard long.

In central California, where the Pomo were the chief "minters," the beads were made from clam shells largely collected at Bodega Bay in Sonoma county.

The shell was grasped between the thumb and forefinger, and chipped into small, rough discs of varying thickness. These were drilled, sorted by size, and strung on the inner bark of wild cotton or milkwood (Asclepias). Loeb[41] states that after European contact, the Pomo strung their beads on iron wire, but this must have been a very exceptional occurrence.

In any event, the shells were now turned on a lathe, against a damp, flat sandstone, which ground them to a uniform disc shape. Finally, they were polished on a deerskin to impart a beautiful gloss to the surface.

The ordinary bead had a diameter of about a half inch, and was called by the Pomo *ka ya, talea,* or *ghai.* Beads of both larger and smaller size were known, but seem to have been much less common. Powers,[42] in 1873, noted:

"Sometimes discs of *hawock** are made two inches in diameter and half an inch thick, which are rated at one dollar a piece, but such large pieces are seldom seen. The Bear River Indians (Nishinams) are the only ones I have seen who count by the single piece; the others rate it by the foot or yard."

Stearns, writing in 1889,[43] illustrates a bead about the size of a quarter

---

* Clam shell. Although the term *hawock* was and is frequently used to denote the California disc beads, it is actually an Algonquian word.

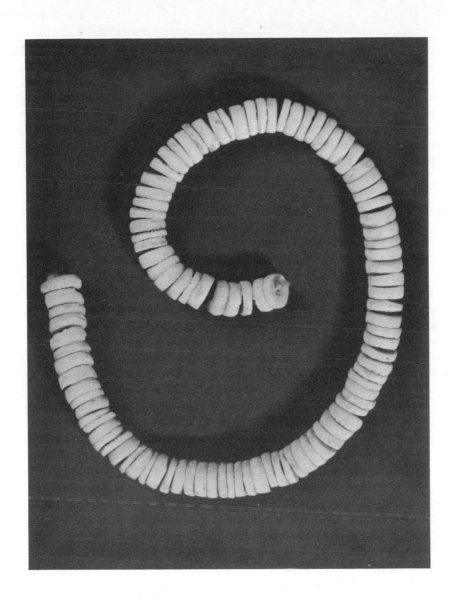

A string of Pomo clam-shell discs, slightly reduced. *Courtesy of the Chase Manhattan Bank Money Museum.*

dollar, and states its value to be twenty-five cents. For the ordinary half-inch diameter size, he gives a value of four cents. He also mentions disc beads of a smaller size. Stearns' valuations must reflect Nishinam reckoning, which also was roughly based on the value of U.S. silver coins of corresponding diameter.

Judging from early reports, it would seem that the value of the clam-shell discs varied considerably from place to place. The Pomo reckoned one hundred and sixty ordinary beads at a dollar, but as the currency moved eastward its purchasing power shot up dramatically.

At the time Loeb wrote (1926), the Pomo supplemented their clam-shell discs with clam-shell cylinder beads. From the thick heel of the shell, long cylindrical beads were made which, according to their length, passed at the rate of twenty to forty common discs. Scraps from the heel were used to make thin cylinders worth four to six of the latter. Scraps from any other parts of the shell furnished discs of smaller than average diameter which, however, were now reckoned at the same rate as ordinary beads. Disc and cylinder beads were strung together according to their kind, and individual beads were only removed when needed for payment.

The Pomo were also the purveyors of that high-value currency made from baked magnesite. The nodules of raw magnesite were buried under a fire, which changed their color from a dull grayish white to beautiful shades of orange. As the material cooled, it cracked into pieces which were then shaped into cylinders, ground, drilled and strung. The Pomo called these beads *po, pol,* or *fol,* and valued a piece of average size (i.e. about two inches long) and of good color and finish at five dollars, or eight hundred common clam-shell discs. Pieces to which handling had imparted a peculiarly fine finish were worth still more.

Kroeber,[44] in considering these beads, thought that "their individual variability in size and quality, and consequently in value, was too great to allow them to be reckoned as ordinary money," though "they were too precious to be properly classifiable as ornaments." He concludes: "They rank rather . . . as an equivalent of precious stones among ourselves."

This is not quite true. In the first place, the magnesite beads are far less variable in size than the clam-shell discs. But even if they were not, the fact could hardly be used as an argument against their monetary status since beads of different size were reckoned at different values. Secondly, the element of quality, as a value determinant, was also present in the case of the clam-shell discs. So, it appears that the only real difference between the two currencies lay in their purchasing power. The high value of the magnesite beads cannot, of course, disqualify them from serving as money any more than it does a large

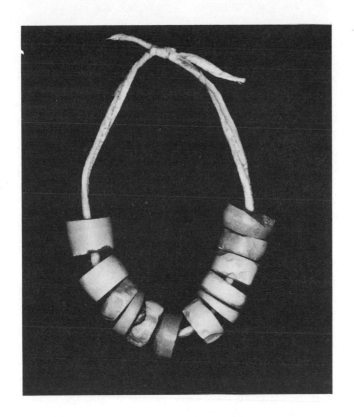

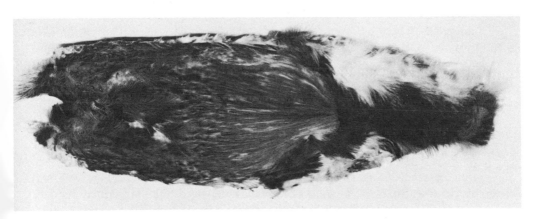

ABOVE: Pomo magnesite beads; BELOW: A woodpecker scalp, one of the exotic currencies of northern California. *Courtesy of the Chase Manhattan Bank Money Museum.*

bank note. Nor does it open the way for a comparison of the former to "precious stones among ourselves," since even diamonds are not used between individuals for payments.

The antiquity of the Pomos' currency may, perhaps, be inferred from its prominent place in one of their creation myths.[45] The story takes place prior to the age of Man. Black Hawk had gone to fetch food for Coyote (the chief protagonist of the creation cycle) who lay sick and starving. In order to reach "food village," the former had to cross Gualala river, and for this purpose he built a raft. Before embarking, however, he withdrew a long string (two lengths) of common clam-shell discs, broke it, and cast the loose beads into the water. Having sacrificed to the river, he commanded his raft: "Now I want you to float well on this water." Despite this, the logs of his raft soon came apart, and he was obliged to build another. This time, Black Hawk built a sturdier raft, and when it was completed he offered four lengths of ordinary beads and repeated his wish. Again, however, the raft disassembled. Black Hawk now fashioned it for the third time and, when he sacrificed to the river, he offered in addition to the four lengths of common beads, four lengths of "large and very fine beads" (magnesite?). Lo, the offering was accepted, and he sped across the water.

Observers from the time of Martinez on, allude to the addiction of the coastal Indians to a gambling game involving the use of small sticks. With variations, the game seems to have been played by Indians throughout North America. In its simplest form, one player hid the sticks in one or the other hand, while his opponent tried to guess which. Among the Pomo, the game was called *witcli,* and is the subject of one of their most amusing tales. As the story opens, a player had just lost all of his currency beads and retired to the mountains. There he disguised himself as a deer and waited. During the evening, he was accosted by a Gilak (a large, supernatural man, with wings, claws and feathers) who, with unaccustomed kindness, attempted to feed him. The Gilak tried in every way to get the deer to eat. He offered him grass, pepperwood boughs, and even stones, but all to no avail. Finally, he offered him shell beads, and with that the deer avidly began to eat. Satisfied that he could provide for the deer, the Gilak carried him off into the sky. There, in his aerial home, he regularly plied his pet with disc beads, and the latter gobbled them down with gusto. Before long, however, the deer's appetite grew so ravenous that the poor Gilak was impoverished. Sadly he returned his pet to earth. Now, as soon as the Gilak departed, the man doffed his deer costume, and made a bee-line for the village where, as usual, a game of *witcli* was in progress. He immediately joined the play, and, armed with the Gilak's lucky money, won continuously.

Another story, recorded by Powers, tells how the magnesite deposit at White Buttes was discovered by a coyote, or rather by a man who had been changed into a coyote because of his sins. Presumably we have here the germ of an historical event, though, as usual, it appears through the veil of a Coyote story.* Since proto-Coyote had taught men all the arts and crafts, it was expected that every important discovery would somehow redound to his credit. In this instance, it was contrived by changing the discoverer *into* a coyote. For this, however, he had first to become an arch villan, since it was only as dire punishment that one was transformed into, or reborn as, an animal. Thus, we find that, immediately on discovering the deposit, that is to say on having served his etiological purpose, the coyote's "hair and his tail dropped off his body, he stood up on his hind legs, and became a man again."

According to the observations of Stephen Powers, purchases among the Pomo sometimes took a curious turn:

"They use an absurd custom of hospitality which reminds one of the Bedouin Arabs. Let a perfect stranger enter a wigwam, and offer the lodge-father a string of beads for any object that takes his fancy—merely pointing to it, and uttering never a word—and the owner holds himself bound as an Indian gentleman to make the exchange, no matter how insignificant may be the value of the beads. Ten minutes later he may thrust him through with his javelin, or crush in his temple with a pebble from his sling, and the by-standers will account it nothing more than the rectification of a bad bargain."

For the Miwok, an inland tribe east of San Francisco, currency was a mélange of peregrinating beads from the far north and not too distant south. There were, in addition, two indigenous currencies made from the shells of the haliotis and olivella.

The former, according to Stearns, was known as *iihl-lo,* or what we commonly call abalone. The shells were usually cut into oblong strips of from one to two inches in length, depending on their curvature. These were drilled at one end, polished to a beautiful iridescence, and hung as pendants, edge to edge. Ten strips of a given kind were strung together. Strips 1¼ by 1 inch were reckoned at a dollar each, and narrower pieces in proportion. Those lacking the coveted iridescence, and thus of little use in adornment, were discounted. Stearns mentions "a couple of fragments I picked up in an old Indian camp . . . worth 25¢ each." Round abalone pieces were also known, and it seems probable that they were valued according to the value of U.S. coins of similar diameter size.

---

* In Pomo mythology, Coyote has several aspects. In one, he is the Demiurge, a helper in the Creation, and the progenitor and instructor of men. In another, he represents mankind itself, and is thus invested with all the human frailities.

Abalone strips, a currency of the Miwok Indians of California. *Courtesy of the Chase Manhattan Bank Money Museum.*

Maidu and Nishinam girls. The first wears a necklace of abalone strips, the second a number of strings of clam-shell discs. Both have headbands and belts decorated with smaller abalone pieces. *Courtesy of the U. S. Bureau of Ethnology.*

The currency status of abalone has been challenged by certain writers who prefer to regard it as a favorite barter item. As concerns the greater part of the Pacific Coast, this view is undoubtedly correct. But in the area under discussion, abalone strips were divided and reckoned in a way which would only be useful to a currency, and there is every evidence that they were accepted as such, albeit as a somewhat less convenient and less popular form than the clam-shell discs.

The other indigenous currency of the area consisted of olivella shells which had been ground down at the top to permit stringing. These were called *kol kol,* and strung, mouth to mouth, in a double row which sometimes reached fifteen feet in length. Being readily available, olivella shells were reckoned at only one fifth the value of common clam-shell discs.

At Mendocino, California (which can be located on even a small map because it is the westernmost portion of the state), the currency use of magnesite beads, clam-shell discs, abalone pendants and olivella shells all came to a close. Circulating in their place were the tusk-shaped dentalium shells, most of which had worked their way south from Vancouver Island. As a result of this long migration, their value and desirability were greatly enhanced. The extraordinary preoccupation of the Yurok Indians with dentalia was vividly described by Kroeber in 1925. Quoted, in part, by Quiggen, it is nevertheless worth repeating here:

"They are firmly convinced that persistent thinking about money will bring it. Particularly is this believed to be true while one is engaged in any sweat-house occupation. As a man climbs the hill to gather sweat-house wood*— always a meritorious practice, he makes himself see them along the trail or hanging from fir trees eating the leaves. When he sees a tree that is particularly full of these visioned dentalia, he climbs it to cut its branches just below the top. In the sweat-house he looks until he sees more money shells, perhaps peering at him through the door. When he goes down to the river he stares into it and at last may discern a shell as large as a salmon, with gills working like those of a fish. Saying a thing with sufficient intensity and frequency was the means of bringing it about. A man often kept calling 'I want to be rich' or 'I wish dentalia' perhaps weeping at the same time. Young men were recommended to undergo these practices for ten days at a time, meanwhile fasting and exerting themselves with the utmost vigor and not allowing their minds to be diverted by communication with other people, particularly women. They would then become rich in old age."

---

* The "sweat-house" was actually a purification lodge. Only greenwood could be used, and it had to be cut in a special way.

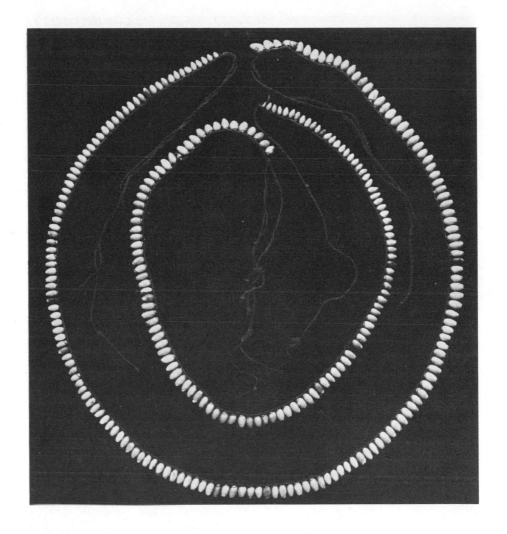

Pair of olivella shell necklaces, reduced. The outer string measures 42½ inches in length. *Courtesy of the Museum of the American Indian, Heye Foundation.*

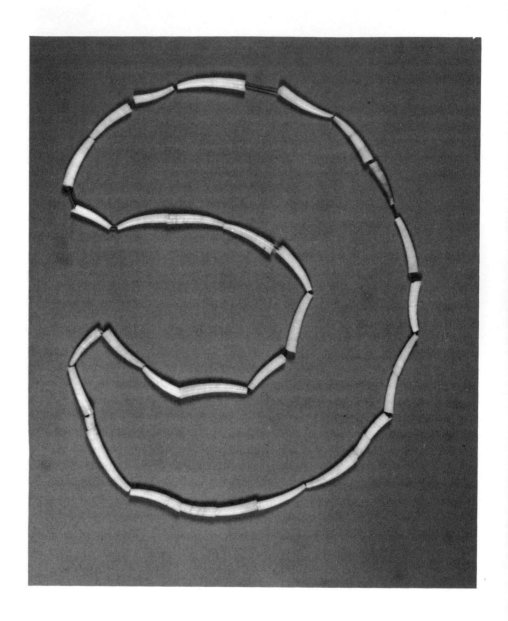

A string of dentalium shells, slightly reduced. This popular currency circulated from northern California to Alaska. *Courtesy of the Chase Manhattan Bank Money Museum.*

Throughout the area, from Crescent City to Eel River, dentalium shells were called *allicotsik* (meaning literally in Yurok "Indian money") ·or just plain *tsik*. The Yurok strung them in lengths of twenty-seven and a half inches, and valued them exactly according to their size. The value increased so sharply in proportion to the increase in shell size that the string with the least number of shells was worth twenty-five times as much as that with the most. Kroeber gives the following table of values:

Size per shell	Value per shell	Number per string	Value per string
1–7/8″	.25	15	2.50
2″	.50	14	5.00
2–1/8″	1.00	13	10.00
2–5/16″	2.00	12	20.00
2–1/2″	5.00	11	50.00

Shells only one-and-a-half inches long served as small change, shorter ones as "squaw money," that is, mere ornaments. Deer sinew was used for stringing, and the dentalia were arranged with opposite ends facing to avoid slipping into each other. To facilitate reckoning, male Indians tattooed the inside of a forearm with lines indicating the length of the different shell standards. This system seems to have grown out of the more primitive and arbitrary one of measuring a string from the thumb tip to the shoulder, and individual shells by the creases of one's left hand.

Powers gives the Karok scale as twenty-five cents to two dollars. More likely, it was the same as used by the Yurok. That Powers did not observe the five-dollar size dentalium is understandable, since they were excessively rare. Indeed, the owner of two such strings was a local hero, and would not part with more than one even to purchase a high-born wife.

According to Powers, the standard measurement among the Hupa was a string of five shells, which was worth from two to ten dollars.

The Shasta, and certain other tribes, engraved their dentalia with fine lines and angles, and wrapped the shells spirally in narrow strips of snake or fish skin. A tuft of feathers from the crest of the red-headed woodpecker might be used to decorate the end. Such niceties showed a reverence for the currency, but did not enhance its value.[46]

Nevertheless, red-headed woodpeckers contributed to the currency of a number of northern California tribes, especially the Karok. The reason is given in a folk tale of the related Pomo tribe.[47]

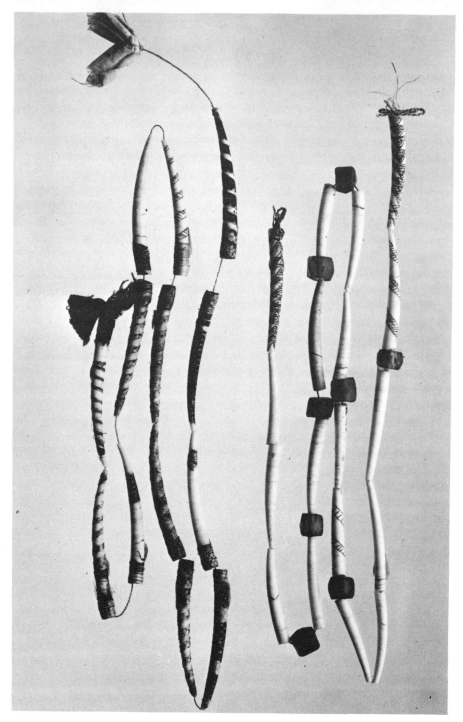

Strings of dentalia, decorated with incised lines and coils of snake skin. The additions, though aesthetic, did not enhance the monetary value of the shells. *Courtesy of the Museum of the American Indian, Heye Foundation.*

A Hupa woman decked out in a large number of dentalium strings. *Courtesy of the U.S. Bureau of Ethnology.*

It seems that in primeval times, when people were still birds, Karrack, the red-headed woodpecker, complained to his feathered friends about the loss he inevitably suffered during molting seasons. Accordingly, it was decided that his molted feathers should be woven into a headband, the devising of which was left to Karrack himself. From this time on, woodpecker feathers have always been preserved for their value.

For the purpose of valuation, two species of woodpeckers were distinguished, the *kokoneu* and the *terker'it*. The former was somewhat larger and more brilliant, and was ordinarily valued at twice the latter. Among the Yurok, however, *kokoneu* passed at one dollar to a dollar-and-a-half, while *terker'it* was only worth ten to twenty-five cents. As of 1872, the Karok valued the scalps at five and two-and-a half dollars respectively.

Another currency of Northwestern California was obsidian blades. These were valued according to color, whether black or red, and thereafter according to their length and nicety of finish.[48] Medium-sized black blades passed at about a dollar an inch, while the ratio lessened somewhat below the length of six or eight inches, and increased sharply above that of about fifteen inches. A good blade twenty inches long would seldom be paid out for fifty dollars, while one thirty inches long was invaluable. Red blades were rarer than the black, and worth at least one-and-a-half times as much. They are almost never found longer than eighteen inches, though reported, in a description of a Yurok dance, as reaching twenty-two inches. Strings of very small blades are also known, and enjoyed monetary use.

Even more valuable were the *ne-gam,* or blades of white flint. These could not be chipped quite so evenly as obsidian, but were worked into a broad and somewhat thinner shape.

The Indians were extremely reluctant to part with large obsidian blades, or even to display them or reveal their whereabouts. Sometimes a man neglected to confide in his own family, and, with his death, the treasure was irrevocably lost.

Among the Hupa, Yurok, Karok and Klamath, very large blades were always carried in the important White Deerskin Dance. Consequently, they were regarded as a kind of tribal property, and the disposal of one by its owner was certain to cause general displeasure. For this reason, they remained virtually priceless, and served more as a store of value than a currency. But this was not true of blades of average size, which were frequently used in commercial transactions.

The use of money by the Yurok in ritual, bride price and indemnification is well documented, and fairly well represents the customs of the northwestern California area. The price of a bride might be paid for entirely in dentalia,

ABOVE: Elk's horn purse, used by the California Indians to hold shell currency. BELOW: Obsidian blade, reduced, an exclusive currency of aboriginal northern California. *Courtesy of the Museum of the American Indian, Heye Foundation.*

String of small red obsidian blades, used by the Karok Indians as currency. *Courtesy of the Museum of the American Indian, Heye Foundation.*

but it usually included deer skins, an obsidian blade, strings of disc beads,* and woodpecker scalps. The exact price was determined by the girl's social status rather than by her beauty. In point of fact, each person in Yurok society had his or her own special value, which was reckoned according to the social standing of the family. Thus, even when brothers exchanged their wives, they did so in two separate transactions.

Powers amusingly describes the plight of the indigent suitor:

"When a young Indian becomes enamoured of a maiden and can not wait to collect the amount of shells demanded by her father, he is sometimes allowed to pay half the amount and become what is termed 'half married.' Instead of bringing her to his cabin and making her his slave, he goes to live in *her* cabin and becomes *her* slave."

Yet, it was far from a laughing matter. The husband, once he had paid in full, in no-wise regarded his purchase as symbolical, and, if anything, was inclined to over-exercise his proprietory rights. Indeed, the detailed Yurok regulations for settlement in the case of wife-killing suggests that it was not an altogether uncommon occurence.

If a man killed his wife by accident, her kin were not entitled to compensation, but payment in full was required in the case of murder or manslaughter due to intoxication. The father-in-law, on receiving the payment, would scrutinize each item and demand to know its history. This ascertained, he could, if he wished, reject anything that had passed down through the bridegroom's family, and insist that it be replaced. Kroeber explains this as follows:[49]

"The reason for the rejection was that blood-money had not been acquired through 'prayer' or magical seeking by fasting, gathering sweat-house fuel, and concentration of wishes, which in Yurok belief is the normal cause of wealth being acquired. As no natural person would wish to 'pray' to receive money by the death of a relative, blood-money would lack the beneficient installation which ritual seeking imparted to normal wealth. Quite likely also, there was fear that the slayer and his kin had 'tainted' the money with evil wishes or practices directed against the family of the person whom their hatred had caused them to slay."

In order to conclude the settlement equitably, both sides would employ *wego,* or arbiters, whose fee was one large dentalium shell each. The arbiters could not be chosen from among one's kinsmen, and were expected to be impartial. Each side was represented by an equal number. Once a settlement had been reached, and restitution made, the avenger relinquished any right to

---

* Though they had no currency status in upper California, the clam-shell discs were still considered valuable, and included in the bride price.

retaliate, and was not even supposed to harbor a grudge against the slayer. It is even said that when a settlement was reached expeditiously, and without haggling, the parties were as likely as not to again become boon companions.

Tribal wars were likewise resolved by blood-money payments, the victor as well as the vanquished being fined. Each slain or injured person was accounted individually, on the basis of their social standing. Compensation for a wealthy victim was more than for a poor one, and, in the case of a woman, the same as her bride price. Since warring tribes could not be reconciled without a full reciprocal restitution, it was always the victor who suffered the greatest financial loss. It seems to me that this principle might be profitably imposed on the warring nations of our so-called civilized world. If nothing else, it would cause a reappraisal of the philosophy of "body count."

Among the Karok, a woman's skills were also considered when determining her bride price. Other than that, courtship followed the same pattern as it did among the Yurok. Negotiations were initiated by the young man who, without any preliminaries, went to the girl's father and made an offer of so-and-so-many strings. This was followed by what, in any other context, would be called "horse trading." Of course, the father enjoyed the advantage, and he knew it. For the more a man paid for his wife, the more valuable she was considered, and hence the greater his own status. "A wife is seldom purchased for less than half a string," Powers informs us, "and when she is especially skillful in making cornbread, and weaving baskets, or belongs to an aristocratic family, she sometimes costs as high as two strings—say $80. or $100."

For a marriage to be legal and binding, the wife had to be purchased in this manner. If she were not, the couple were considered outcasts and the children illegitimate.

According to Powers, an average Karok blood-payment was one string of dentalia. Moreover, there was no adultery so flagrant "but the husband can be placated with money; and it seldom requires more than one string." Insults could be as devastating as murder. The worst offense, indeed, the most heinous crime, was to utter the name of another's deceased relation. This caused the mouldering skeleton to turn over in its grave and moan. Such a cruel act required the same compensation as did murder, and, if not paid in dentalia, was held accountable in blood.

Dentalia were also used to atone for a religious trespass, as, for example, when one inadvertantly beheld the sacred smoke emerging from the sweat house. For this offense, the priest demanded shells to the amount of twenty, thirty or forty dollars, depending on the circumstances.

Since the acquisition of wealth was largely a matter of invocation and volition, it is not surprising that the two great ceremonial dances of the Yurok and neighboring tribes were largely dedicated to this purpose.* In order to fortify their petition, the dancers bedecked themselves with various forms of wealth and money.

The White Deer-skin Dance was an exclusive ritual in which only upper class Indians could participate. In the center, the leader of the dance carried a deer skin on a pole, and at each end performers marked time and gesticulated with a large flint. The blade was tied tightly with a buckskin string, which looped around the wrist to prevent any slipping.

On the tenth day of the dance, the performers brought out their greatest treasures: white deerskins and the longest flint and red obsidian blades. Now the dancer wore a whole deerskin, the nose of which was decorated with red-headed woodpecker scalp feathers and abalone pendants. For this information, as well as that which follows, we are indebted to Mrs. Lucy Thompson, a high-born Klamath woman.[50] Mrs. Thompson tells us that:

"All of the dancers have great rolls of shell beads [dentalia], called *Turktum* strung around the neck, hanging down over the breast and reaching to the waist. These shells are the same species of shells as *cheek,* only they are shorter, and do not have the value by from fifty to one hundred times as much, and all have headdresses but no feathers, only the one bald eagle or other eagle feather that is stuck in the back of the hair and stands up perpendicular. The four men that stand at the end of the row of dancers and which carry the large flints . . . have for a headdress a close woven cloth, decorated with tusks or teeth of the sea lion."

Following the tenth day, the dancers returned home for more provisions, and, on the next, they resumed. During the final two days, the dance was held in a sacred enclosure where only the highest-born were allowed to go. This particular dance could be performed no more often than once every two years.

Even more wealth was displayed at the Lodge dance, the most sacred ceremony of the Klamath and neighboring tribes. Unlike the deerskin dance, this was a public ceremony in which could participate every class of Indian, rich and poor, noble and slave. Here,

"They take the scalp of the woodpecker, which they sew together from sixty to one hundred in number, on a piece of nicely dressed buck skin; the edges also being such skin; it looks like a plug hat. They let the ends hang as streamers at the back of the head. These are valued at from one to two hundred dollars, having red and white fringes, which make them look very

---

* This will seem less strange when it is realized that these dances were originally World-renewal rites which were necessary to maintain the wild plants that sustained the people. Such was their original wealth, and much of its symbolism was later transfered to money.

Lodge Dance performed by the Hupa Indians of California. Each performer wears a headdress of woodpecker scalps and numerous necklaces of dentalia, and in his right hand holds a deer-skin mat. *Courtesy of the Museum of the*

pretty. These headdresses are called *Rah-gay* and the scalps are called *cheese* whether one or many of them. They have great strings of the long, hollow shells, called *cheek* and *turk-tum,* around their necks, hanging down over the breasts to the waist. . . . Now the last two days of the dance commence, and the finest dresses and the most valuable of articles are used; all the riches are brought out, showing which are the most wealthy of families, some of which have long records dating back for generations."

So pervasive was the symbol of wealth during these festive days, that even by-standing children could be distinguished according to their class. Thus, the off-spring of wealthy families would bedeck themselves with dentalia of, or nearly of, monetary size. Those from less fortunate families wore strings of shorter shells, or of broken dentalia which were called *wetskak.* And finally, there were the children of intermarriages, who could be recognized by their necklaces of pine nuts.

10. The Northwest Coast

The early traveller, proceeding northward from California, would soon notice a distinct change in the monetary situation. Of those media to which he was accustomed, only dentalium, which had originated in the north, survived as a currency. As in California, the shells were valued according to their size. However, the northwest coast unit of measurement was the fathom, equal to six feet. The Chinook traders of the Columbian Valley, who were as celebrated for their commercial enterprise as for their jargon, called the shells *hiaqua,* and this name came to be generally adopted. Dunn, referring to the Chinook system, said:[51] "Forty to the fathom is supposed to be the fixed standard of excellence and worth; for instance forty which make a fathom are worth nearly double fifty which make a fathom."

To qualify as *hiaqua,* no more than twenty-five shells could make up the fathom. Smaller shells were strung together with broken and inferior* ones, and collectively called *kop kop.* They were worth only a fortieth the value of *hiaqua,* and used for small change.

The Chinook greatly favored dentalia as ornaments, and women used strings of the shells to tie their braids. Other strings were suspended from the nose or ears, which had been pierced or slit for the purpose of holding them. This, it appears, rendered the Chinook even more unsightly to European eyes than did their practice of depressing their skulls. Jewett observed:[52]

---

* Dead shells, washed ashore, and lacking the customary milky whiteness.

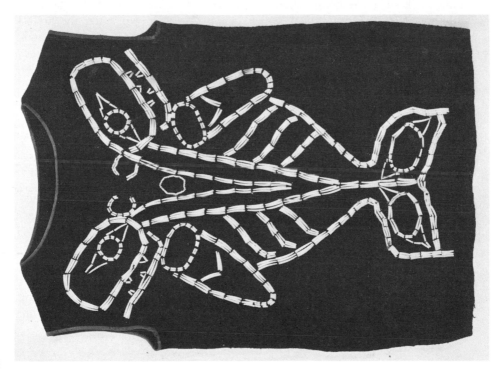

Haida shirt and blanket, the first decorated almost exclusively with dentalia, the second with dentalia and abalone strips. *Courtesy of the Museum of the American Indian, Heye Foundation.*

"Some of these girls I have seen with the whole rim of their ears bored full of holes, into each of which would be inserted a string of these shells that reached to the floor, and the whole weighing so heavy that to save their ears from being pulled off they were obliged to wear a band across the top of the head."

Early writers disagree on the method used to procure dentalium shells. For example, Dunn writes:

"They are . . . caught in Nootka Sound, and along Vancouver's Island:— a piece of deer flesh, or of fish, is dropped from a line to the bottom: this they cling to; and they are then drawn up, and carefully gutted and preserved."

I think it is evident that Dunn never witnessed the operation. A more detailed and reasonable description is given by artist Paul Kane, who travelled through the area around the middle of the nineteenth century.[53]

"Yellow-cum is the wealthiest man of his tribe.* His property consists principally of slaves and ioquas [hiaqua], a small shell found at Cape Flattery, and only there, in great abundance. These shells are used as money, and a great traffic is carried on among all the tribes by means of them. They are obtained at the bottom of the sea, at a considerable depth, by means of a long pole stuck in a flat board about fifteen inches square. From this board a number of lone pieces project, which, when pressed down, enter the hollow ends of the shells, which seem to be attached to the bottom by their small ends. The shells stick on the pieces, and are thus brought to the surface. They are from an inch and a half to two inches in length, and are white, slender, and hollow, and tapering to a point; slightly curved, and about the size of an ordinary tobacco pipe stem. They are valuable in proportion to their length, and their value increases to a fixed ratio, forty shells being the standard number to extend a fathom's length; which number, in that case, is equal to a beaver skin; but if thirty nine be found large enough to make the fathom, it would be worth two beaver skins; if thirty eight, three skins; and so on, increasing one beaver skin for every shell less than the standard number.

"Yellow-cum presented me with a pair of ear ornaments of these shells, consisting of seventy or eighty shells in each."

John R. Jewett, in his own narrative, described two methods for procuring the shells:

"A piece of wood a foot square is filled full of little pegs, which are sharpened to a fine point. This block is fastened to a long pole, and thrust down into the water till it reaches the shell-fish, and the sharp points enter the hollow shells, breaking them from their hold on the bottom, and bringing them to the

* The Makahs of Cape Flattery, just below Vancouver Island.

surface. Another method described to me by the Indians is to tie a large piece of seal or whale meat to a pole, and press that down firmly on the shells, which, becoming imbedded in the meat, are easily broken off, and thus secured. I, however, have never seen the operation, and therefore cannot speak positively on the subject."

The first of Jewett's methods is that to which Kane alluded, and which he more clearly described. The implement used to impale the detalia was simply a form of rake. The other method is apparently what Dunn had heard about but not fully understood. The use of blubber was not to elicit a carnivorous response, but, by its extreme softness, to permit impaling by the sharp round end of the shell. Since this method was described to Jewett by the Indians themselves, we shall have to accept its historicity. However, it does not seem to have been much employed, for neither Kane, nor J. K. Lord, whose description follows, refer to it. Lord's account confirms that of Kane, and adds a number of interesting details about the operation.[54]

"An Indian when shell-fishing arms himself with a long spear, the haft of which is a light deal; to the end of it is fastened a strip of wood placed transversely, but driven full of teeth made of bone. The whole affair resembles a long comb affixed to the end of a stick with the teeth very wide apart. A squaw sits in the stern of the canoe, and paddles it slowly along, whilst the Indian with the spear stands in the bow. He stabs this comb-like affair into the sand at the bottom of the water, and after giving two of three prods draws it up to look at it. If he has been successful perhaps four or five money shells have been impaled on the teeth of the spear. It is a very ingenious mode of procuring them, for it would be quite impracticable either to dredge or net them out, and they are never, as far as I know, found between tidemarks."

Writing of the Vancouver Island Indians in 1857, W. C. Grant mentions dentalium belts, but states that the currency use of the shells had largely declined in the area.[55] Nevertheless, dentalium remained, for at least some time afterwards, the predominant currency of the more inland tribes.

Richardson refers to the currency use of both dentalium and arenicola (a genus of crustacean worm) shells among the Kutchin Indians of the Yukon.[56] Affluent Indians commonly wore layers of necklaces, broad belts of shells around the shoulders and breast, and narrower bands around their forehead and ankles. Other shells were woven along the seams of their leggings.

The gradual decline of dentalium as a currency of the northwest coast was due not to any influx of specie, but to the growing traffic in two other articles, one coveted by the White man, the other by the Indian. These were, respectively, furs and blankets.

Furs were the first to supplant the precious dentalium, but their rapid

extinction as a currency, at least among the Indians, was a foregone conclusion. Indeed, the desire of the coastal Indians to amass wealth required the
adoption of a currency that could be hoarded in great quantities. The pressure
of the European's own commercial appetite rendered furs an impractical
choice, and, as a result, blankets soon became the Indian's currency unit and
medium of exchange.

*   *   *

Had North America given rise to civilizations like those of the Aztecs and
Incas, it is virtually certain that France and England would have plundered the
very source of wealth that later placed our nation on a firm financial basis.
Even so, the Europeans found, in the cold and inhospitable northern forests,
an article almost as valuable as gold and silver. The Indians, for their part,
were unacquainted with the artificiality of European values, and bartered away
quantities of their most precious pelts for trinkets and other cheap commodities. Needless to add, both English and French plied their trade with avidity.

Dunn provides us with a picturesque description of the way in which the
early Europeans and Indians conducted their trades:

"Hordes of Indians would come down at stated periods, in a squadron of
light canoes, laden with beaver skins and other spoils of their year's hunting
—unload their canoes—draw them on shore—form an encampment outside
the town—dispose their goods in order, and open a kind of fair with all the
grave ceremonial so dear to the Indians. An audience would be demanded of
the Governor-general: he would respond to the application, and hold the con-
ference with befitting state, seated in an elbow chair; whilst the Indians were
ranged in semi-circle before him, seated on the ground, and silently smoking
their pipes. Speeches would be made,—presents exchanged, and the audience
would break up in good humour.

"Then the work of traffic would commence with great activity; and all
Montreal would be alive with naked Indians, running from shop to shop,
bartering their commodities for arms, knives, axes, kettles, blankets, and
various other articles of use or fancy, on all of which the merchants realised
enormous profits as there was no money used in their early traffic; every
transaction being conducted by barter in kind."

As of 1830, the Tlingit, a coastal tribe of Southern Alaska, was using sea-
otter skins as currency. Subsequently, however, caribou supplanted sea otter
for this purpose. Krause, writing in 1885,[57] tells us that fifteen to twenty caribou skins could purchase a slave, five to six a sea otter, and ten to fifteen a
good canoe.

Among the Kutchin Indians of the Yukon, the standard was a large beaver skin called a "skin." However, payments could be made in a number of articles, whose values were fixed in terms of the skin.

In such a system, can beaver legitimately be called a currency? I believe the answer must be "yes." First of all, the existence of a multiplicity of media is no justification for denying them all currency status. This is especially true when they are related items such as furs. One could cite, by way of analogy, our own multi-metallic system, especially during its operation under the gold standard. Of course, if every item under the beaver standard had possessed a fixed value, and stood on an equal footing with every other, we would be dealing with a moneyless system. But such was not the case.

By the mid-nineteenth century, made-beaver was not only the European's standard of value in the northern Yukon, but was everywhere accepted in payments. It was, as Henry Mobery of old Fort Edmonton summed it up, "the currency of the country."[58] The real question, then, is not whether one should consider *beaver* a currency,* but whether to extend the status to guns, bullets, shot and blankets, which also had fixed values, and were sometimes used in payments. Blankets, as I have already mentioned, served as a currency among the Northwest Coast Indians. But beyond this, and the fact that shot was briefly used in seventeenth century Massachusetts, I prefer to designate these latter items as "favored barter items," so as to distinguish their *popular* usage from the *established* usage of beaver. I have no doubt that persons well-stocked, or over-stocked, in guns, etc. would have requested payment in beaver or other standard currency.

The situation among the Indians was somewhat different. In the early days, the White man did not regularly venture into the interior, but waited for the Indians to sally forth, as they did, periodically, with large quantities of furs. The chief purveyor was the Chinook, who dominated the Columbia River route, and obtained much of its stock from tribes in the interior, from whom it would otherwise exact a toll for the right of passage.

Gradually, however, the situation changed. This was due, first to the *Coureurs des Bois,* or Rangers of the Woods, who, in accompanying the Indians on their hunting expeditions, acquainted themselves with remote tracts. These men then set out for Montreal, and through a combination of hunting and trading, obtained what furs they could. The French government prohibited their activities, but when the licensing system was relaxed, the Rangers were often employed to work on a percentage basis.

* Its monetary use was so firmly established, that copper beaver-shaped tokens were issued by the Hudson Bay Co., and circulated at the value of one skin each. I have been told that silver specimens also exist.

July 14th. 1703.
Prices of Goods

Supplyed to the

𝕰𝖆𝖘𝖙𝖊𝖗𝖓 𝕵𝖓𝖉𝖎𝖆𝖓𝖘,

By the feveral Truckmafters ; and of the Peltry received
by the Truckmafters of the faid *Indians.*

ONe yard Broad Cloth, *three* Beaver skins, *in feafon*.
One yard & half Gingerline, *one* Beaver skin, *in feafon*
One yard Red or Blew Kerfey, *two* Beaver skins, *in feafon*.
One yard good Duffels, *one* Beaver skin, *in feafon*.
One yard& half broad fine Cotton, *one* Beaver skin, *in feafon*
Two yards of Cotton, *one* Beaver skin, *in feafon*.
One yard & half of half thicks, *one* Beaver skin, *in feafon*.
Five Pecks Indian Corn, *one* Beaver skin, *in feafon*.
Five Pecks Indian Meal, *one* Beaver skin. *in feafon*.
Four Pecks Peafe, *one* Beaver skin, *in feafon*.
Two Pints of Powder, *one* Beaver skin, *in feafon*.
One Pint of Shot, *one* Beaver skin, *in feafon*.
Six Fathom of Tobacco, *one* Beaver skin, *in feafon*.
Forty Biskets, *one* Beaver skin, *in feafon*.
Ten Pound of Pork, *one* Beaver skin, *in feafon*.
Six Knives, *one* Beaver skin, *in feafon*.
Six Combes, *one* Beaver skin, *in feafon*.
Twenty Scaines Thread, *one* Beaver skin, *in feafon*.
One Hat, *two* Beaver skins, *in feafon*.
One Hat with Hatband, *three* Beaver skins, *in feafon*.
Two Pound of large Kettles, *one* Beaver skin, *in feafon*.
One Pound & half of fmall Kettles, *one* Beaver skin, *in feafon*
One Shirt, *one* Beaver skin, *in feafon*.
One Shirt with Ruffels, *two* Beaver skins, *in feafon*.
Two Small Axes, *one* Beaver skin, *in feafon*.
Two Small Hoes, *one* Beaver skin, *in feafon*.
Three Dozen middling Hooks, *one* Beaver skin, *in feafon*.
One Sword Blade, *one & half* Beaver skin, *in feafon*.

*What fhall be accounted in Value equal
One Beaver in feafon : Vt.*

ONe Otter skin in feafon, is one Beaver
One Bear skin in feafon, is one Beaver,
Two Half skins in feafon, is one Beaver
Four Pappcote skins in feafon, is one Beaver
Two Foxes in feafon, is one Beaver.
Two Woodchocks in feafon, is one Beaver.
Four Martins in feafon, is one Beaver.
Eight Mincks in feafon, is one Beaver.
Five Pounds of Feathers, is one Beaver.
Four Raccoones in feafon, is one Beaver.
Four Seil skins large, is one Beaver.
One Moofe Hide, is *two* Beavers.
One Pound of Caftorum, is one Beaver.

Early eighteenth century bulletin pricing goods sold to the Indians in relation
to the beaver skin. *Courtesy of the Hudson Historical Bureau.*

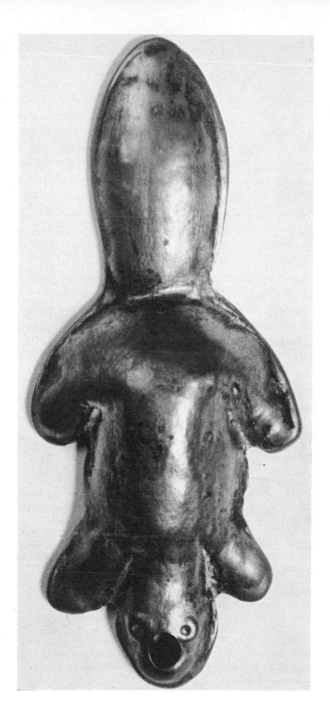

Copper beaver effigy, used as a token in the early fur trade, and equal in value to one beaver pelt. Actual size is 1 by 2½". *Courtesy of the Museum of the American Indian, Heye Foundation.*

With the conclusion of the French and Indian War, in 1763, the British monopolised virtually the whole of the North American fur trade. The powerful Hudson's Bay Company did not normally send its men into the interior, but smaller companies and groups still followed the example of the Rangers. Finally, in 1805, after a protracted internecine rivalry, the various small companies merged together to form the Northwest Company. Unlike the Hudson's Bay Company, the latter made a regular business of dispatching agents into the interior, with the result that Indians everywhere in the north were awakened to the immediate negotiability of furs, and particularly of beaver.* Among some tribes, furs in general served as currency, while, as with the Whites, beaver was the standard of value. This seems to have been the situation in central Alaska, for Bancroft states:

"At Nuklukahyet, where the Tananah River joins the Yukon, is a neutral trading ground to which all the surrounding tribes resort in the spring for traffic. Skins are their moneyed currency, the beaver skin being the standard; one "made" beaver-skin represents two marten-skins."

As earlier stated, the overriding desire of the northwest coast Indians to accumulate their chosen form of wealth made furs an impractical choice. Nevertheless, the fur trade indirectly led to a solution by causing the Indians to stockpile an enormous number of European woolen blankets. By the mid-nineteenth century, these had become both the standard of value and principal currency of the area.

Between 1849 and 1850, for example, Hudson's Bay Company bought two hundred square miles from tribes in Vancouver Island for the price of

---

* A prologue to the American fur trade is contained in the Icelandic Vinland Sagas,[59] which describe Thorfin Karlsefni's encounter with American Indians about the year 1010 A.D. Karlsefni was the brother-in-law of Leif Eiriksson, and the first Greenlander to attempt to colonize North America. Judging from the Vinland map authenticated by Yale University a few years ago, as well as by the persistent references of the Norsemen to grapes, Karlsefni must have been somewhere in Maine. During the first summer, a group of Indians (Micmacs?) came to his settlement with various furs which they bartered for red cloth (or, as in the alternate version, for milk). Early the next winter, a similar transaction took place. Were the pre-Columbian Indians then already trading furs among themselves? Perhaps, to some extent they were, but in as much as this group brought nothing else with them, it seems likely that they had seen the Norsemen trapping, and thus felt reasonably sure that their pelts would be acceptable. The account will have a familiar ring to all who are acquainted with the later stories of barter between Europeans and Indians. It reads: "What the natives wanted most to buy was red cloth; they also wanted to buy swords and spears, but Karlsefni and Snorri forbade that. In exchange for the cloth they traded grey pelts. The natives took a span of red cloth for each pelt, and tied the cloth around their heads. The trading went on like this for a while until the cloth began to run short; then Karlsefni and his men cut it into pieces which were no more than a finger's breadth wide; but the Skraelings [*i.e.* savages] paid just as much or even more for it."

nine hundred and fifty blankets. Among these same Indians, blood payments could always be rendered in blankets, unless the victim was from the chief's own family. Kane, writing of the Chinook in 1859, observed that twelve blankets could purchase a sea-otter skin (the most precious skin on the coast), and two a gun.

Among the Kwakiutl, and presumably neighboring tribes also, the unit was a cheap white woolen blanket, which was reckoned at fifty cents. A double blanket had the value of three single ones. The circulation of blankets, as well as of other wealth, was enlivened by two means. The first was gambling, an activity at which the northwest coast tribes excelled even the Pomo. "During the progress of the [stick] game," wrote Kotzebue of the Tlingit,[60] "they present a perfect picture of melancholic stoicism. They lose at this game all their possessions, and even their wives and children, who then become property of the winner."

The other means was the potlatch. Now, with all due respect to anthropology, I can think of no better definition for "potlatch" than Elizabeth Barrett Browning's line, "a gauntlet with a gift in it." The potlatch was just that, a challenge hurled through the medium of a gift. At its greatest, it was an extraordinary affair, involving, as its combatants, the pillars of Northwest Coast society. The potlatch was not, however, an isolated event, the mere response of anger to a sense of injury. It was rather the main event in an arena of perpetual competition from which there was no escape. The principle on which the competition was based was reciprocal giving. That is to say, one gave gifts to one's rival, who, on accepting them, was obligated to make a larger return. If he could not afford to accept them, he was disgraced.

As an alternative or supplement to barter, gift-giving is not an unusual economic device. It differs from barter primarily in that payment is deferred, and from a credit system in that it is not regulated with regard to time or to media. Moreover, it is prestige, not profit, that is at stake in each transaction. When, instead, a profit is sought, out-and-out plundering is resorted to, and may be quite socially acceptable even though trading for the same purpose would be considered mean and degrading.

Like barter, gift-giving can very well accommodate itself to a currency system, and supplement it to a great extent. To appreciate this fact, we have only to look at our own society where gift-giving functions on an almost ubiquitous if subterranean level in procuring services from those who cannot overtly sell them. The five-dollar bill that is given to the neighborhood postman or policeman, or the five thousand dollar donation to the campaign fund of a sympathetic politician, are instances, small and large, of the principle in operation. (Here, however, we have added a perjorative element which is absent in its role among primitive societies.)

The Illiad and Odyssey, with their vivid delineation of an ancient warrior society, are replete with examples of reciprocal giving. Like the Northwest Coast Indian, the Homeric hero never tires of telling us about great gifts given and received, and, indeed, beyond physical prowess his status depended on the amount of treasure he could and did dispense.

Prior to Colonial rule, the psychological aspect of Northwest Coast society may have fairly well resembled that of the Greeks depicted by Homer. Afterwards, however, with the compulsory adoption of more peaceable pursuits, the unusual aggressiveness of these Indians must have been sublimated and found an outlet in the more socially acceptable potlatch. This, at least, would explain the fundamentally hostile character of their reciprocal giving. In the Homeric world, while the pursuit of personal glory was not less keen, the indispensable means to attain it was combat. Gift-giving created and maintained alliances, and served as a means of mutual help. On the Northwest Coast, the more beneficial aspects of the mechanism, if they existed previously, were virtually extinguished during Colonial times.

From the cradle, life was a preparation for the potlatch. At birth, Boas tells us,[61] a boy was simply given the name of his locality. He received his second name after a year, at which time some relation would present a paddle or a mat to each member of the tribe. When coming of age (at ten to twelve years), he received his third name, but, for this, he himself was obliged to distribute gifts to his clan or tribesmen. To accomplish this, he accepted blankets from other boys in the tribe, which loans he had to repay after a year at one hundred percent interest.

However, as he received his own gifts back at two hundred percent interest, he actually began his adult life with a credit of one hundred blankets. For the rest of his days, he was engaged in amassing wealth so that he could compete with the rival selected for him in a different tribe. To this end, he could borrow blankets from members of his own tribe, always, of course, at one hundred percent interest. By judicious borrowings and lendings, he could, in time, become wealthy, and therefore influential. Rivalry within one's own tribe was "outrivalled" by that involving an alien tribe, but every Indian was ultimately competing against every other.

Of the great articles of wealth, *i.e.* slaves, canoes, and shields (generally called "chief's coppers" for want of understanding of their use) the last-named were the most coveted, and hence supremely valuable. Writers, when referring to these shields, have usually characterized them simply as "property," but Boas, who pioneered in Kwakiutl ethnology, considered them to be the equivalent of high-denomination notes. I am inclined to accept this view, though, admittedly, it requires some explanation. The value of a shield was at any time established, but since it changed with each transaction, the purchasing power of every one was different. The shields were really like so many interest-bearing notes, each with its own record of earnings.

A shield normally increased in value every time it was given away, but if, out of need, it were spent, it was discounted by fifty percent. Revaluations, it is true, might be arrived at with ceremonial haggling, but, as they were ultimately dictated by the weight of precedent, they were by no means arbitrary. Moreover, once the new value was established, it was always recognized. So, fluctuations apart, one can say of the shield that its value was fixed. Certainly, the shield was never refused in payment, and, since, in historical times, it had no other use, it cannot but have a legitimate, if somewhat individualistic, claim to monetary status.

When a wealthy man wished to heighten his own prestige at the expense of his rival, he would offer the latter a shield. Failure to accept the offer was a tacit admission of the inferiority of the entire rival tribe, since it meant that the latter had not, collectively, enough wealth for the purpose. Boas gives a wonderfully graphic account of the potlatch that ensued when a rival accepted the challenge, and tried to turn it to his own account.

"The trade is discussed and arranged long beforehand. When the buyer is ready, he gives to the owner of the copper [shield] blankets about one-sixth of the total value of the copper. . . . The owner of the copper loans these blankets out, and when he has called them in again, he repays the total amount received, with 100 per cent interest, to the purchaser. The prescribed preceeding is as follows: The buyer offers first the lowest price at which the copper was sold. The owner declares that he is satisfied, but his friends demand by degrees higher and higher prices, according to all the previous sales of the copper. . . . Finally, the amount offered is deemed satisfactory. Then the owner asks for boxes to carry away the blankets. These are counted five pairs a box, and are also paid in blankets or other objects. After these have been paid, the owner of the copper calls his friends—members of his own tribe— to rise, and asks for a belt, which he values at several hundred blankets. While these are being brought, he and his tribe generally repair to their house, where they paint their faces and dress in new blankets. When they have finished, drums are beaten in the house, they all shout 'hi!' and go out again, the speaker of the seller first. As soon as the latter has left the house, he turns and calls his chief to come down, who goes back to where the sale is going on, followed by his tribe. They all stand in a row and the buyer puts down the blankets which were demanded as a belt, 'to adorn the owner of the copper.'

The whole purchase is called 'putting the copper under the name of the buyer.'

"In this proceeding the blankets are placed in piles of moderate height, one pile close to the other, so that they occupy a considerable amount of space. In Fort Rupert there are two high posts on the beach bearing carved figures on top, between which the blankets are thus piled. They stand about 40 steps apart.

"On the following day all the blankets which have been paid for the copper must be distributed by the owner among his own tribe, paying to them his old debts first, and, if the amount is sufficient, giving new presents. This is called 'doing a great thing.'"

In the more spirited competitions that took place between chiefs, property was destroyed instead of given away. This utter disregard of one's possessions was the supreme indication of wealth, power, and a strong mind. By failing to destroy an equal amount within a short period of time, a rival was disgraced. A particularly aggressive challenge was delivered by the breaking of a shield. This was done at the great grease feast to which the rival had been invited for the express purpose of humiliating him. The grease, or fish oil, was offered first to the rival who, if he considered the feast inferior to his own, refused the spoon and ran out of the house to fetch a shield. On returning, he would strike the various house posts with his shield, unless the host had taken the precaution of tying to each a shield of his own. Striking a post was considered equal to slapping the host's face, and hence a great insult. Once it was done, the rival would break a larger shield and return to his antagonist the fragments of both pieces. As a rule, the shield was not broken all at once, but in sections, the dismembering taking place over a number of "transactions." The T-shaped ridge was the last part to be given away, and its value was reckoned at two thirds that of the whole shield. If the fragments of a broken shield were bought back and riveted together, the piece was worth even more than previously, being a visible record of one's largess.

Still more prestigious than giving one's rival a shield, was throwing it in the river. This indicated that one did not even require compensation. Interestingly, the first shield of which we have an historical record was found on Copper River. Capt. Urey Lisiansky, who, in 1804, observed the discovery, later recorded:[62]

"Mr. Baranoff bought with him also two other curiosities: one of which was a thin plate, made of virgin copper, found on the Copper River, to the north of Sitca: it was three feet in length, and twenty-two inches in breadth at one end, and eleven inches at the other, and on one side various figures were painted. These plates are only possessed by the rich, who give for one of them twenty to thirty otter skins. They are carried by the servants before their

Kwakiutl chief's "copper," or ceremonial shield. *Courtesy of the Chase Manhattan Bank Money Museum.*

Kwakiutl chief holding a broken ceremonial shield. From an old photograph by Frank Boas. *Courtesy of the Smithsonian Institution.*

master on different occasions of ceremony, and are beaten upon, so as to serve as a musical instrument. The value of the plate depends, it seems, in its being of virgin copper: for the common ones do not bear a higher price than a single skin."

In Boas' time, a wealthy chief owned as many as two or three dozen shields, and after his death the sum of his wealth was carved on his mortuary column. On occasion, the shields themselves were nailed to the grave posts.

There has been much useless speculation over the origin of the chief's copper, which I have throughout referred to as a shield. Considering that the Northwest Coast Indians are known to have used shields, that the chief's coppers would have been admirably suited to serve as such, that one surviving specimen has a gripping loop on the back, and that at least one other shows the effect of a ricochetting bullet, the question should really be considered settled.*

With the curtailment of warfare, the shields inevitably took on a quasi-ceremonial character, eventually becoming, as the Haida say, "property above all else." The collecting of shields by the powerful and affluent may have originated in trophy hunting, even as the Homeric heroes, at great risk to themselves, would pause on the battlefield to remove and claim the armor of a fallen opponent.

The quality of the shield was very important, and could be determined by striking it and listening to the sound. A shield fashioned by the natives in their own way resounded with a dull sound, while those which the Europeans afterwards counterfeited "rang." The latter were soon discounted by ninety-five percent or more. And here, I think, we have the reason why shields were "carried by the servants before their master on different occasions of ceremony, and are beaten upon, so as to serve as a musical instrument." Far from there being any aesthetic purpose, a shield was beaten to provide an audible demonstration of the owner's wealth.

---

* The argument that most other American tribes used round shields is no more valid than it would be with reference to the ancient Greeks among whom both oval and round shapes are encountered. Again, the Northwest Coast carvings which show obviously non-militant figures carrying shields, and gripping them at the edges, were doubtless made at a later date, when the shields had already assumed the character of ceremonial property.

11. Moving Eastward

In the early days, the aboriginal money of California enjoyed a wide market. Clam-shell discs circulated in the south as far as Arizona, and the Pima Indians, below Tuscon, would accept nothing else. The Navahos, to the south of Parrot City, Colorado, used olivella shells. By the later nineteenth century, however, these had become very scarce, and Indians would frequently scrounge around the ruins of old buildings, looking for the shells. A small string of olivella was then sufficient to buy a good horse.

Dentalia and abalone discs seem to have made their way even farther east, for Lord writes:

"It is quite clear, and also a very curious fact, that the *hiaqua* and *kop kop* were known and used by the Indians of the interior at some distant period, although no trace of their use or knowledge of the shell exists at present; for in digging out some flint implements, stone beads and other things I need not here enumerate, from the drift, I found numbers of dentaliums and round buttons made of the Haliotis nacre. The distance from the nearest seaboard was about 1,000 miles, and the language spoken by those inland Indians incomprehensible to the Indians of the Coast."

In all probability, the shells had been current more recently than Lord suspected. Their disappearance, like that of the olivella in certain regions, was due to the gradual replacement of indigenous California currencies by U.S. coins, and this did not take place until the latter part of the nineteenth century. Of course, the shells would have disappeared first of all from the

Freckled Face, an Arapaho woman, wearing a dress decorated with elks' teeth, a common Indian currency in Idaho, Montana and Wyoming. *Courtesy of the Museum of the American Indian, Heye Foundation.*

interior, but even this is not likely to have happened before the nineteenth century. Indeed, dentalium was still so highly valued in the Dakotas that U.S. traders found it desirable to obtain the shells from eastern importers. Writing of the Gros Ventre Indians, Matthews states:[63]

"It seems probable that they once carried on a trade indirectly with the tribes of the Pacific Coast, for they had dentalium shells similar to those obtained on the Pacific, and they prized them so highly that the white traders found it advisable to obtain them for the trade. As late as 1866, ten of these shells of inferior size, costing the traders only a cent apiece, would buy a superior buffalo robe, and formerly only two or three of the same quality were paid for a robe. Modern traders with whom the writer has conversed, obtain their shells from eastern importers, and know nothing of the supply. They suppose them to come from the Atlantic Coast or the Great Lakes, and call them 'Iroquois shells,' which is probably their corruption of the Chinook *Hyakwa,* but it is possible the reverse is the case."

During the late nineteenth and early twentieth centuries, wapiti or elk's teeth, were a common currency in Idaho, Montana and Wyoming. Their use was specifically noted among the Shoshone, Bannock and Crow tribes, but probably extended to others also. This is the only verified example of tooth currency of which I am aware for the Americas, though many examples might be cited for the Pacific Islands. As in the case of the New Guinea dogs' teeth, only the canine teeth of the elks were used. In 1890, their current value was twenty-five cents each.[64]

Among the Crow, the teeth were strung, or sewn in large quantities on women's clothing, and a prospective husband was expected to own enough to decorate his wife's best dress.[65] As late as 1926, one hundred teeth could purchase a good horse.

After the discovery of gold in California, gold dust became a common medium of exchange. The smallest denomination in use was the "pinch," that is, the amount one could raise between his thumb and forefinger. Equal to twenty-five cents in silver coin, the pinch soon gave rise to a spirited competition between buyer and seller. The former would add a quantity of ground brass to the gold in his satchel, and the latter moistened his fingers and dug in until his adversary really "felt the pinch!"

A more sober approach was occasionally adopted by assayers, who weighed out gold grains in even dollar denominations, and wrapped them, like medicine powders, in small papers. It has been observed of the Alaska gold rush at the turn of the present century that some of these packets circulated unbroken over a period of years.[66]

12. Roanoke and Wampum

We have seen that various types of shells and shell beads were already serving as currency in the western United States in pre-contact days. Most of these early beads were discoid, which at once facilitated their drilling, and permitted them, when strung together, to be worn comfortably. Excavations in the middle west, and even in the east, have produced similar beads, and since those whose use survived into historical times are known to have served as money, it seems likely that the same situation obtained elsewhere. As late as the eighteenth century, long after they had been supplanted in the north by wampum, disc beads known as *rawrenock* (though frequently corrupted by the English into the more familiar and easily pronounced "roanoke") were still circulating on the south Atlantic coast.

William Strachey, writing about 1612,[67] defined *rawrenaw* as a "chain of beads." If we equate *ock* with *hock,* which is an Algonguian word for shell, the meaning is clear enough.

In 1714, Lawson[68] recorded that some English smiths had attempted to make Indian shell money, but that it was so time-consuming "nothing could be gained . . . especially in making their *ronoak,* four of which will scarce make one length of their wampum."

Somewhat more information was given by Beverley in 1722:[69]

"The Indians had nothing which they reckoned Riches, before the English went among them, except peak [i.e. wampum], roanoke, and such like trifles made out of the Cunk shell. These passed with them instead of Gold and

107

Silver, and served them both for Money, and Ornament. It was the English alone that taught them first to put a value on their Skins and Furs, and to make a Trade of them."

After briefly describing wampum, he adds:

"They have also another sort which is as current among them, but of far less value; and this is made of the Cockleshell, broke into small bits with rough edges, drill'd through in the same manner as beads, and this they call Roanoke, and use it as the Peak."

Woodward,[70] writing in 1880, assumed that *rawrenock* was simply a "variety" of wampum. In 1949, Slotkin and Schmitt[71] went a step further, and described a reference made in 1608 to "roanoake" as "the earliest reference on the use of wampum as money." This view is not, however, sustained by Beverley's account of the beads, nor by any other data that we have concerning their use. It is true that until, perhaps, the mid-seventeenth century, disc beads are much more in evidence than wampum on Iroquois sites, and that even after this time they still turn up, sometimes in both purple and white. Moreover, in order to communicate certain ideas, the Algonquian decorated strings of these beads with colored feathers, which practice must inevitably remind us of wampum. But for all this, there is no evidence that the Iroquois, who invented wampum, ever used disc beads in the same overall capacity, nor that among non-Iroquois tribes the older currency ever attained to the all-embracing ritual importance of wampum.

The term "wampum" is a corruption of the Algonquian *wampumpeage,* which denotes "a string of white shell beads." Hodge breaks it down as follows:[72] *wamp* = white; *umpe* = a string (of shell beads); *ag* (or, alternately, *ak*) = the plural form. From this, it is evident that the generic use of "wampum" to include purple beads is incorrect. The Indians, of course, had a separate term for the latter, which they called *suckauhock.* Here the derivation is somewhat different; *suc* = dark, and *kauhock* (or, alternately, *kauhog*) = clam, the mollusc whose shell was used in its manufacture.

The English, who were never a nation to respect the *lingua franca* of non-Europeans, indiscriminately used *wampumpeag,* "wampum," and "peag" or "peak" to denote both the purple and white beads. Such, however, was the weight of the White man's usage, that, by the nineteenth century, the term "wampum" was everywhere current among the eastern Indians. Thus we have the curious philological phenomenon of the once proud Iroquois referring to their own sacrosanct invention by a European corruption of an Algonquian word!

When the Dutch arrived in Long Island, they found that the Indians called it *sewhounhocky,* or "land of the loose shells." The colonists shortened

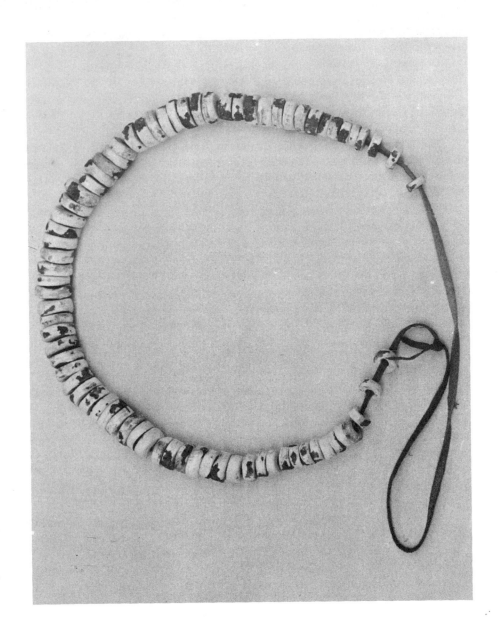

A string of clam shell beads, or "roanoke," the aboriginal currency of Virginia.
Courtesy of the Chase Manhattan Bank Money Museum.

the term to "sewan" (or, alternately, "sewant"), and in this form it had the same generic usage as did wampum in New England.

Ironically, no Iroquois term for wampum ever became current among the Europeans. Hodge gives *oneko'r'ha* for the Mohawks, and *otko'a* for the Onondaga and Seneca, but does not say whether the terms are generic. Morgan[73] likewise mentions *otekoa,* but states that it refers only to the small white council beads of the Iroquois.

The earliest known references to North American shell beads is found in the journal of the French explorer Jacques Cartier[74] who, in 1535, encountered an Iroquian-speaking people, presumably the Huron, at Montreal. He writes:

"The most precious article they possess in this world is *esnoguy,** which is as white as snow. They procure it from shells in the river in the following manner. When an Indian has incurred the death-penalty or they have taken some prisoners in war, they kill one and make great incisions in his buttocks and thighs, and about his legs, arms and shoulders. Then at the spot where this *esnoguy* is found, they sink the body to the bottom, and leave it there for ten or twelve hours. It is then brought to the surface; and in the above-mentioned cuts and incisions they find these shells, of which they make a sort of bead, which has the same use among them as gold and silver with us; for they consider it the most valuable article in the world. It has the virtue of stopping nosebleeding; for we tried it."

Lescarbot, writing in 1609,[75] equated the *esnurgni* with wampum, but noted that it was no longer in use in the area visited by Cartier.**

"This [wampum] it is which the people of the great river of Canada in the time of Jacques Cartier called *esnurgni* . . . a word which I have had great difficulty in understanding, and which Belleforest misunderstood when he tried to speak of it. To-day they have no more of it, or else they have lost the art of making it; for they greatly use the *matachias* [ornaments] which are brought them from France."

From Lescarbot's time down to our own, most writers have taken this view. Slotkin and Schmit, whose 1949 article contains the last major discussion of the subject, states: "The earliest reference to what is presumed to be wampum are those by Cartier from the Northeast culture area." Unfortunately, neither archeology nor the Indians' own traditions bear this out. Disc

* Usually translated as *esnurgny* or *esnurgni.*

** In 1595, the Iroquois had driven out and nearly destroyed the Huron people which Cartier encountered. When Lescarbot arrived, the area was uninhabited except for bands of Algonquians, who passed through in the course of their warlike forays.

beads do indeed turn up in pre-contact Huron grave sites, but the same cannot be said of wampum.* Moreover, Iroquois legends persistently maintain
that wampum was invented by Dekanawida or Hiawatha in connection with
the founding of the Iroquois League (*ca.* 1570). Whatever *esnurgni* was
then, it does not appear to have been wampum. Most probably (and this is
supported by archeological finds in the area) it was a discoid bead similar to
the *rawranoke* of Virginia and Carolina. Indeed, Charlevoix, writing in 1744,
tells us:[76]

"James Cartier in his memoirs makes mention of a shell of an uncommon
shape, which he found, as he says, in the island of Montreal; he calls it
esnurgni, and affirms it had the virtue of stopping a bleeding at the nose.
Perhaps it is the same we are now speaking of [wampum], but they are no
longer to be found in the island of Montreal, and I never heard of any but
the shells of Virginia which had the property Cartier speaks of."

Beauchamp, whose monograph on wampum[77] is considered the most
authoritative, found Cartier's story "strange" and seemingly "absurd." As "a
practical naturalist, acquainted with the forms and habits of all New York
and eastern Canadian fresh-water snails," he coud think of none with the
carnivorous inclinations attributed to the *esnurgni*. More recently, however,
certain of the ostensibly herbivorous snails from this region have been proven
to be omnivors, a fact which would seem to fully absolve Cartier's statement.

Not only that, but the same macabre technique of obtaining *esnurgni* is
described, albeit mythologically, in a Huron legend. The Huron of Lorette,
among whom it was current, were descendents of the ancient Huron of Ontario, whom Cartier encountered. The legend tells us that wampum originated
from the bodies of sorcerers who were conquered by the first missionary
priests, and cast into the lake to drown. Due to an exudation of magic matter
brought about by defeat and death, the sorcerers' bodies were afterwards
found to be covered with the shells.

Admittedly, it is doubtful whether wampum was ever made from shells
obtained in this manner. But since wampum supplemented the ancient *esnurgni,* and was probably identified in the Huron mind with the latter, the
discrepancy is not of much importance.

Let us now leave *esnurgni, rawranoke* and the whole genre of disc beads,
and turn our attention to the origin of wampum.

Slotkin and Schmitt, in a rather extraordinary concluding statement,
tell us:

* Barrel-shaped beads, from the 2nd century A.D., have been found in a serpent
mound in Peterborough county, Ontario, but they are not known there in late prehistoric
or historical times.

"It should be emphasized that the evidence is too fragmentary to reach certainty. The fact that the Dutch material provides us with 1626 as a *terminus ante quem,* suggests that a more intensive study of all Spanish, French, English, and Dutch records before that date is needed if we are to come to definite conclusions about the early use of wampum."

It is a curious perversity which makes some scholars loathe to examine the traditions of the very people they are studying. As though primitive societies were incapable of saying anything worthwhile about themselves, and only the judgments of foreign adventurers, who knew not even the aboriginal language, had value!

The Iroquois have always claimed credit for the invention of wampum, and so it is not surprising that they should have the largest tradition concerning it. This includes historical legends as well as folk tales. Both in their own way tell us that wampum was invented contemporaneously with, and for the purpose of assisting in, the formation of the Iroquois League.

According to the lifetime research of J. N. B. Hewitt,[78] the League was founded about 1570, following many years of intense effort on the part of Dekanawida and his disciple, Hiawatha. Although most persons would readily profess a familiarity with the latter, the Hiawatha "immortalized" by Longfellow's poem was actually Minabozho, an Ojibwa deity. The diverse Iroquois traditions are themselves a little confusing, not so much as to *what* took place as to *whom,* in each instance the action should be referred. My own remarks are based directly or indirectly on Hewitt's admirable reconstruction.

Sometime around the first quarter of the sixteenth century, there was born among the Huron a child named Dekanawida. Many miracles are related in connection with his life. Dekanawida is said to have been born of a virgin mother who, on learning through revelation that her child would prove a curse to the people, resolved to drown him. Thrice she tried to do so, but, inexplicably, he was always restored to her arms. Finally, her maternal love prevailed, and she submitted to what now seemed the inexorable will of Fate.

Years passed, and Dekanawida matured, becoming a celebrated prophet and statesman. When, exactly, he left his people and journeyed south is unknown. From the warnings he afterwards gave the Iroquois about the coming of the "white throats," it would seem almost certain that he was still among the Huron when Cartier arrived. Hewitt believed that the formation of the Iroquois League might have taken as long as thirty years, and, assuming Dekanawida left the Huron soon after observing Cartier, this figure would not be too far off.

Hiawatha, who was formerly an Onondaga, had left his own tribe because of atrocities committed by Dehadodao, his brother and a ranking chieftain.

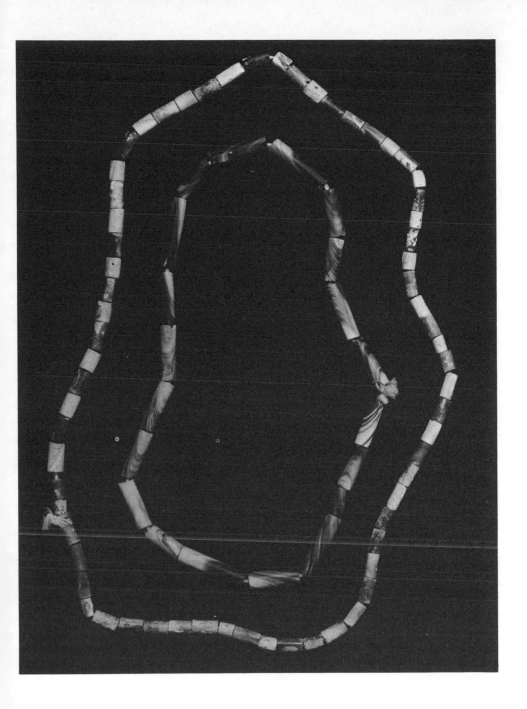

Wampum. A mixed (purple and white) string of the usual sort surrounding a string of the long Campbell beads. *Courtesy of the Chase Manhattan Bank Money Museum.*

For some reason, the latter so detested Hiawatha that he had murdered his entire family. Either out of fear, or as an exile, Hiawatha left the Onondagas, and sought refuge among other of the tribes. Finally, he was accepted into the Mohawks, whereupon he remarried and raised a second family.

As yet, history gives little indication of the coming greatness of Hiawatha. In fact, when he next appears, it is under hardly flattering circumstances. It seems that Hiawatha, still a cannibal according to the custom of the tribe, chanced upon a stranger, killed him, and prepared for his meal. Unbeknownst to himself, however, he was observed by Dekanawida, who silently followed him back to his lodge. Dekanawida then climbed to the roof of the lodge and peered down the smoke hole. Directly below, Hiawatha was boiling water in which to cook his victim. Suddenly, he saw in the water the reflection of a human face. The effect was so traumatic that then and there Hiawatha renounced cannibalism. Still dazed, he wandered out of the lodge and into the forest. There he received a second shock in the person of Dekanawida. For a long time the two men spoke together, and, as the disciple grew more receptive, the prophet unfolded his dream for human brotherhood.

Like Moses, Dekanawida was to take a group of wrangling tribes and weld them into a nation. Like Moses, he was to set before them a higher law than that to which they were accustomed. And finally, like Moses, Dekanawida had an impediment*, and chose another to speak for him to the people.

The cornerstone of the plan was the confederation of the Iroquois tribes. For, as Dekanawida prophesied: "When the White Throats shall come, then if you are divided, you will pull down the long House, cut down the Tree of Peace, and put out the Council Fire."

To effect and retain such a union, it was necessary to devise some non-violent means of settling tribal and intertribal disputes. Retaliation would have to give way to compensation. In order to emphasize the ritual importance of the payment, and thus insure its acceptance, Dekanawida introduced wampum.

I have mentioned the Iroquois belief that wampum was unknown until introduced by Dekanawida. Its original use is suggested by the following legend.

Dekanawida, we are told, was approaching the village of the Mohawks. When he was just close enough to be observed, the prophet seated himself on the ground and began stringing wampum. His unusual actions were soon reported to the chief, who sent a party to investigate. When the men returned,

---

* Since, in both instances, the prophet had been brought up among a different people, the "impediment" was probably a language difficulty.

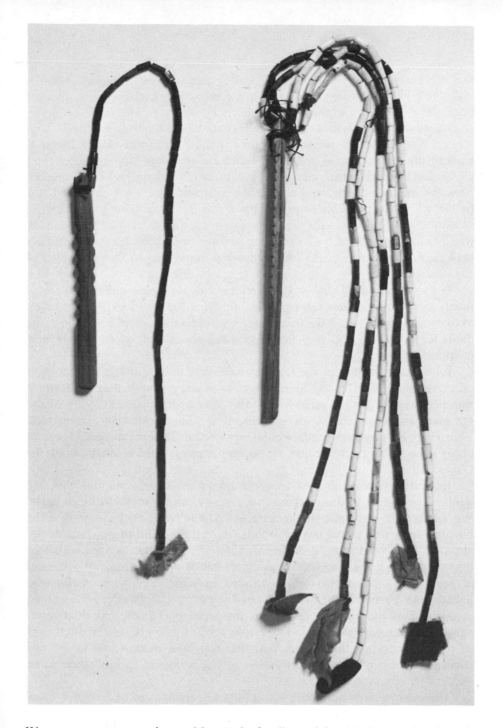

Wampum message strings with notched talley sticks (slightly reduced). AT LEFT: Seneca string used to notify councillors of impending meeting. AT RIGHT: Five Onondaga message strings, exact purpose unknown. *Courtesy of the Museum of the American Indian, Heye Foundation.*

and confirmed the earlier report, the chief's curiosity was aroused. Accordingly, he asked them to go again, and invite the stranger to a council. They at once obeyed, but lo, Dekanawida, on receiving the invitation, made no reply. In fact, he did not even look up, but merely continued to string his beads. The request was repeated a second, and then a third time, whereupon Dekanawida finally responded by giving his wampum string to the emissaries, and explaining that their chief must reciprocate before asking him to a council. Now the Mohawk chief, on receiving the gift, was somewhat chagrined, for he had no wampum of his own. Finally, he made up an invitation string by substituting wooden sticks for the beads. This was then offered to Dekanawida who graciously accepted both the string and the invitation. Thus, the prophet held his first council with the Mohawks, and introduced to them the idea of confederation.

It should be added that wooden sticks and porcupine quills were commonly used for invitation among many northern Indian tribes. In fact, even in historical times, both have occasionally served as wampum substitutes, the quills for invitation, and the sticks for messages as well as for I.O.U.'s in payments.

As for the meaning of the legend, there is, I think, no great difficulty if one does not try to be too literal. It tells us very simply that the earliest wampum was used in the same way as the older invitation sticks. Very likely, wampum was soon afterwards introduced in council meetings themselves. Thus, step by step, the beads would have acquired a sacrosanct character until, at last, they had become the virtual cement with which to bind the Confederation.

Interestingly, a number of Iroquois myths associate wampum with the quills of a fabulous bird, sometimes, specifically, with a mythical black eagle. We are told, for example, that a certain Iroquois chief, on learning that the bird had been seen in the nearby woods, offered the hand of his daughter to any man who could bring it down. Many were the arrows winged with that hope, but though the bird was occasionally hit, it merely threw off a shower of wampum (*i.e.* feathers) and continued its flight. Finally, a youth, who hailed from an unfriendly tribe, stepped forward and asked permission to compete. This was angrily opposed by the warriors, but the old chief intervened and granted the request. The arrow sped to its mark, the bird fell, and its plumage enriched the people. With the marriage, peace came to the two tribes, and the youth taught them how to use wampum to bind their vows and heal all grievances.[79]

The association of wampum with plumes or quills is to be found in other legends also. One of these concerns the reconciliation of Hiawatha with his murderous brother, Dehadodao. As fate would have it, it was Dehadodao who most bitterly opposed the idea of confederation. Only after the Mohawks, Senecas, Oneidas and Cayugas had all finally agreed, would he grudgingly commit the Onondagas to membership. And even then, it seems to have been necessary to make him first chief of the League.

Such descriptions as we have of Dehadodao are striking. He is said to have made dishes and spoons from the skulls of his enemies, and to have worn a head-dress ornamented with snakes. In the legends, Dehadodao's head-dress gives way to live, hissing snakes, which grow among his hair, and curl around his pipe when he smokes. Hiawatha's ultimate triumph over his brother is portrayed, mythologically, by having the former comb the snakes from Dehadodao's hair with wampum. Since the Indians normally made their combs from porcupine quills, the allusion has significance.

Again, in the Onondaga version of the story I earlier related, Hiawatha sits in front of the Mohawk village stringing not wampum, but black eagle quills. Here also, the chief is unprepared, but he is said to reciprocate with partridge quills.

The principal source of the wampum-bird tradition seems to be the Onondagas, who also state, as a rule, that their first wampum consisted of porcupine quills. Now, it is a fact that porcupine quills, dyed in a variety of beautiful and brilliant colors, were both popular and precious articles among the northeastern Indians. The quills were woven into necklaces, bracelets and belts, and were favorite trade items over a large area. However, when wampum became available, it generally supplanted porcupine quills as a form of decoration, just as it replaced colored sticks for the purpose of invitation. This then would account for the intrusion of porcupines into wampum folklore. But what about the eagle quills?

The prairie tribes are known to have highly valued eagle quills, but they do not seem to have been used in the east, even though, in the old days, treaties could be made by taking oath on the wing of a large bird. Moreover, the eagle of the myths is no ordinary bird, but a fabulous creature, who appears, however unwittingly, as the harbinger of wealth. Altogether then, there seems to be no historical justification for the wampum bird. I suspect that its origin should be sought rather among the tangled leaves of Creation folklore, where a mythic black eagle, or thunderbird, is associated with the fertilizing rains, and, hence, with Man's cereal wealth.

According to the above chronology, the first genuine wampum beads should date from somewhat before 1570 A.D. That a good many of the beads now in museums were made by the aboriginal method is well established, as is the fact that some of these come from pre-contact sites. Admittedly, the number of the latter are few, but this would only indicate that the earliest wampum was not used in burial, but carefully preserved by the tribe.

I suspect that the purple beads are of a slightly later vintage. For one thing, the Iroquois themselves believe that the first council wampum was made entirely from fresh water shells. For another, clam shells were probably unavailable to the Iroquois until after they had confederated and extended their domain. Likely as not, they were the contribution of the Mohawks, who exacted tribute wampum from the Pequot, the latter of whom, in turn, mulcted those great purveyors of clams, the Long Island Indians. Finally, we have the statement of Lescarbot, who, in 1609, wrote of the Micmac and certain other tribes:

"The Brazilians, Floridans, and Armouchiquois [Kennebec] make carcanets and bracelets (called *bou-re* in Brazil and *matachiaz* by our Indians [i.e. the Micmac]), from the shells of those great seashells which are called *vignols* and are like unto snails, which they break in a thousand pieces and gather up, then polish them upon a grindstone; so that they make them very small, and when they have pierced them they make beads, like those which we call porcelain. Among these beads mingle alternately other beads, as black as the others I have spoken of are white, made of jet or of certain hard or black woods which resemble it, which they polish and make as small as they wish, and this has good grace."

13. Wampum in Dress and Ceremony

In their palmier days, the Indians of the Atlantic coast were well supplied with wampum, and used it extensively for adornment. The ladies delighted most in necklaces, sometimes giving them as many as a dozen turns around the neck. Other strings gathered up their shining tresses, or hung from the ears. Still others were made into bracelets to encircle the wrists, or, perhaps, the arms just below the shoulder. Every damsel was decked out according to her means, and even the poorest wore her trifle. As for the affluent, "the women wear a petticoat down midway the leg, very richly ornamented with sewant so that the garment sometimes costs 300 guilders . . . [They] bind their hair behind in a plait, over which they draw a square cap thickly interwoven with sewant." So noted Arnoldus Montanus in 1671,[80] and in his opinion it was all "most sumptuous." Men were less splendidly attired, presumably because of the demands of their wives. But children were given collars of wampum, and chiefs and sachems girdled their waists with wampum belts, or threw them across their shoulder like a scarf. Ordinary belts consisted of twelve rows of one hundred and eighty beads each, but they increased in length and breadth according to the social standing of the wearer.

"Ornament," grieved Shylock, "is but the seeming truth which cunning times put on to entrap the wisest." The Iroquois, however, thought otherwise. That which they flaunted as "a beauteous scarf" was also sanctified as the means of preserving truth. Wampum was at once the witness to a pledge, and the pledge itself, a living record that bound the participants to their words.

119

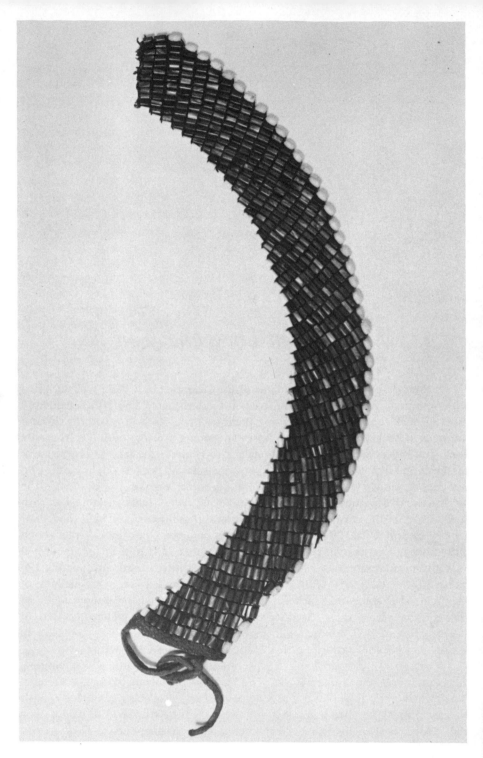

A Penobscot wampum necklace, 13″ long, 1½″ wide, purple with borders of white beads. *Courtesy of the Museum of the American Indian, Heye Foundation.*

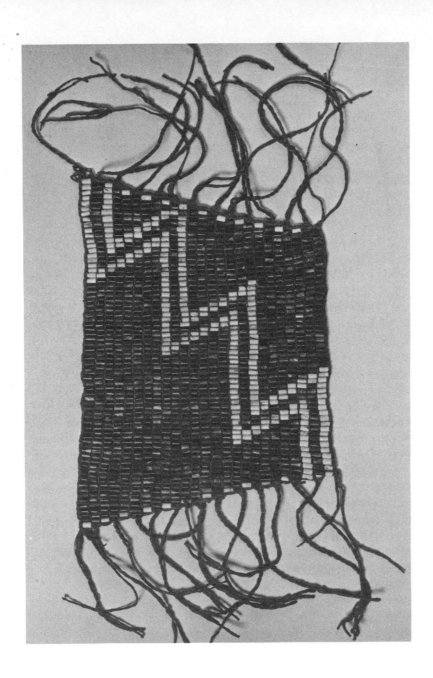

Iroquois wampum armlet, 6½″ by 8″. *Courtesy of the Museum of the American Indian, Heye Foundation.*

As witness, it was held in the hand while one made his pledge. As mnemonic device, wampum, in the form of a belt, or *macequoce,* could be read according to the symbolic arrangement of the beads. But like the Peruvian *quipo,* it could only be understood by a trained reader. It is, moreover, doubtful if even the most skilled readers could decipher a belt without being previously instructed in its meaning.

The wampum reader, who was also the keeper of the belts, was usually a *sachem.* Among the Iroquois, this office was the hereditary privilege of the Onondaga. Wampum belts comprised the only records that a tribe possessed of its treaties, councils and other outstanding events. Thus, at every great council, it was customary for the *sachem* to conduct a reading of the more important belts. Twice a year, in addition to this, he would instruct the most promising young men in the history of their people. From one belt he would recall the daring exploits of their fathers, from another the submission of an alien tribe. In this way, the tradition was handed down, and the sentiments of pride and patriotism were rekindled in the hearts of each generation.

Heckwelder gives the following account of a skillful *sachem:*[81]

"On the manner in which the belts or strings of wampum are handled by the speaker, much depends; the *turning* of the belt which takes place when he has finished one half of his speech, is a material point, though this is not common in *all* speeches with belts; but when it is the case, and is done properly, it may be as well known by it how far the speaker has advanced in his speech, as with us on taking a glance at the page of a book or pamphlet while reading; and a good speaker will be able to point out the exact place on a belt which is to answer to each particular sentence, the same as we can point out a passage in a book."

The first emblematic belt of which we have an unequivocal record was presented at Quebec in 1653 by a New England Indian chief. The arrangement of the purple and white beads showed the road which his Canadian friends would have to follow to visit him. A contemporary Jesuit account quotes the chief as saying:[82] "There are the lakes, here are the rivers, here are the mountains and the valleys that it is necessary to pass. Here are the portages and waterfalls." Of course, the belt did not show all of these things in the manner of a map. The lakes, rivers, mountains, etc. were represented symbolically, and served only as a memory aid to the reader who would later recall what had been spoken over them.

The largest emblematic wampum belt on record was made by the Iroquois in 1756, to invite the remoter tribes to join their Confederacy.[83] "Upon it was wrought the sun by way of an emblem of Light, and some figures representing the Six Nations. It was intended to signify that they now saw objects in their proper light, and that they were fully convinced of the truth of every-thing proposed."

In the early days, communication with or between the eastern tribes was virtually impossible without wampum. "It is obvious," wrote Sir William Johnson in 1753,[84] "to all who are in the least acquainted with Indian affairs that they regard no message or invitation, be it of what consequence it will, unless attended or confirmed by strings or belts of wampum, which they look upon as we our letters or rather bonds."

Though modern wampum readings are, admittedly, not always unim-peachable, the following may be of interest. It was given of a celebrated Onondaga belt in 1898:[85]

"Between Bastable building and the corner of the Genesee and Warren streets, Syracuse, was held the last council which completed the league. Both Hiawatha and Tododaho [Dehadodao] were there.

"Represents an everlasting tree—always growing, reaching to heaven that all nations may see it; and under they set a general fire to burn forever—the council place of the Five Nations—and that the council fire is to be kept at the Onondagas, and the Onondagas are the expounders of the law.

"After they had ratified—it was understood—we look far away and we see a darkness, and in the darkness an unknown and strange face, and they could not understand what it was—and it came to be interpreted that we would be forced to adopt an unknown law—but it was coming before that generation passed away, and finally their heads would roll and roll away, and after a time they would recover their bodies, and then they would embrace the law that was once lost to them, and the tree would grow forever. After they will restore the original law their confederation will be more permanent than the first one, and their original law will remain forever. They say that one of the women said: 'You can use all the water of the ocean to wash away the Indian blood, and when you have done [this] there is as much water left in the ocean as before you began—so the law—you can take from it parts of the Indian law, and put another in its place, but it will come again and last forever.'

"This was the last belt that was made at that ratifying time. When the belt was ready it was said by one of the orators to that council, 'This is the last belt which we make confirming the laws which we have just adopted,' and he encouraged the people of the Five Nations to instruct them with the mean-ing of the wampum to serve the laws. At the conclusion of his remarks, he said, 'As long as you will follow up the laws of the Five Nations you will be in prosperity and happiness, but whenever our people may not heed the in-structions we [are] instructing you, then it will come in the state of dissension among our people—and the last remark—if you will disobey and disregard the laws we have, that generation will suffer.' Hiawatha made that speech.

"This belt is not the original which was there at that time, but a copy. It was made not a great while after the death of Hiawatha. That each clan shall be entitled to one principal chief and war chief. When the council ended, Hiawatha . . . distributed the belts among the clans—making the clans and chiefs. And in this speech he said: 'I have made a place for you under ground and a fishing ground. I have finished my work.' It is claimed that he did not die, but went up in his canoe and said, 'When you shall be in a state of confusion I will come back.'

"That Hiawatha saw the strange face in the midst of the darkness, and he interpreted it that the unknown law which was coming, should prevail over the new law—that is, the law which has just been adopted and the tree that was just planted. The root spread from east to west, and from south to north. Under the tree, while the root of the tree was spreading, all the Five Nations laid their heads on the root. That is the constitution. If any of their enemies should attempt to strike against the root, the man who struck the root would turn, and the blood would come out of his mouth. That is revenge for blood. The roots of the tree would continue spreading in all directions forever; and the fire would continue forever, and the smoke of it all up to heaven, so that all the nations of the world would see; and that the laws—that is the wampums —be read every year forever."

When the message of a wampum belt was especially private in nature, the carrier was requested to take it "underground," that is, to prevent its contents from being known to anyone other than the recipient. Sometimes, it was further stipulated that the former should enter "into the earth," with the message, which meant that he should travel through the woods, avoiding all paths and places where he might be seen. A belt sent by the Iroquois to the Ojibwas, in Canada, in 1694, was accompanied by the following message.[86]

"I put this message between you two underground, where it is to remain three years, in order to say to you that you must think much of the union that ought to exist between us, and not forget that here is your ancient country; that you ought to advise us of the designs of *Ontonio* without letting him know it. Fear not visiting us; you will always be welcome."

Unlike the treaty belts, message belts were normally dismantled, and the beads divided among high-ranking Indians who, in turn, were called upon to furnish beads when a reply was sent. The reply belt was expected to be more or less equal to the first, though a small adjustment was made when the two tribes were of different rank.

Wampum was the harbinger of war as well as an offering of peace and friendship. Among the Iroquois, an invitation to join in war could be delivered by driving into the war post of each village, a tomahawk painted red and decorated with blue wampum. If the matter were to be considered, a belt, predominantly blue, with white figures representing the five nations, and decorated with red paint, was sent to each nation for approval. (By contrast, a peace belt was predominantly white.) This was followed by a grand council at Onondaga, which determined whether war should be prosecuted, and, if so, whether the offending tribe should be annihilated or absorbed into the nation.

On being delivered, a belt was vigorously thrown on the ground. If its proposals, either for war or peace, were accepted, the belt was raised. Otherwise, it was left to lie for hours, or even days.

"Sometimes" Beauchamp notes, "the rejection was vigorous. In 1691, the Five Nations rejected a French belt while at Albany. 'We declare the belt of wampum given by the French venomous and detestable, and did spew it out and renounce it, and will not accept of the belt but prosecute the war as long as we live; and left the belt upon the ground in the court house yard.' In 1693, imperious Count Frontenac kicked away three belts sent him by the Five Nations, and five years later flung a belt in the face of ten Onondaga messengers. They retorted in kind when he sent them five belts in 1699. A sachem asked for them in the council at Onondaga, 'and one of the sachems got them and threw them towards him, but not so far as that sachem sat, and another Indian very scornfully kicked them at him.' Quite as vigorous was the reception of the war belt which [Sir William] Johnson gave in 1756. 'A Seneca chief laid hold of it, sang the war song and danced,' and it passed on to the others."

Today, the two largest collections of wampum belts are, respectively, in the Museum of the American Indian, Heye Foundation, in New York City, and the New York State Museum. The latter collection was acquired, in 1898, from an Onondaga chief named Baptiste Thomas. The exact terms of the transaction have recently been the subject of a warm debate between the Indians and the state authorities. According to the latter, Thomas voluntarily relinquished the belts to the then chancellor of New York University. The chancellor was, at the same time, appointed sachem, and given the title Ho-sau-na-ga-da, or "name bearer." Subsequently, a rather extraordinary law was passed, which made wampum a public record "forever," and empowered the Chanceller to "secure by purchase, suit or otherwise any wampums" that were outstanding. When the Chancellor later relinquished his office of sachem, it was transferred to the director of the state museum.

The last Onondaga chief, George Thomas, sought to reclaim the wampum on the ground that it was only leant to the state. Because of the ever-increasing scarcity of genuine beads, the tribes are now having difficulty in conducting their rites. Perhaps the most eloquent plea that could be made on their behalf is a quotation from former Onondaga sachem, Thomas Webster. In 1888, Webster declared:

"Wampum means nothing to the white man; all to the Indian. There is a tree set in the ground and it touches the heavens. Under that tree sits the wampum. . . . The wampum bearer keeps the treaties of the nation."

Though the most impressive, *machequoce* was only one of the special forms in which wampum was wrought for different purposes. Another, far humbler in appearance, but of the greatest ritual importance, was the "chief's horns," which symbolized deers' antlers. This consisted of a short, forked string of alternating blue and white beads. Horns were the badge of a chieftain, and he wore them at all times, unless he had the misfortune of being deposed, or, as it were, "dehorned." Upon his death, however, the horns were removed, and other beads were used in the burial offering.

The extreme importance attached to this last provision can be inferred from the following injunction in the Iroquois Book of Rites:[87]

"As soon as he [i.e. the chief] is dead, even the horns shall be taken off. For if invested with horns he should be borne into the grave, oh my grandsires, we should perhaps all perish."

That is, it would be like burying the chief's office with him.

Wampum also played an important part in condolences. Purple beads were used for this purpose, and were called *deyunhoughdoyenghdouh*. When a chief or sachem died, all activities in that nation were suspended until the condolence had been completed. The death was announced by a runner, who carried special wampum to each of the other nations. In the case of a principal chief, three strings of purple beads, united at one end, were used. The death of a war chief was announced with a single string, joined at the ends to form a circle. Attached to the condolence wampum was a small stick, indicating by a number of notches how many days remained until the condolence ceremony. When the time arrived, the visitors proceeded part way to the council house, and then lit a fire around which they waited for the mourners. The meeting was followed by songs, speeches, and the return of the invitation wampum. Afterwards, the party proceeded to the council house, where the mourners and the condolers seated themselves at opposite sides of the house, with a curtain separating them. Then, says Beauchamp, who had the opportunity to attend a Tuscarora ceremony:

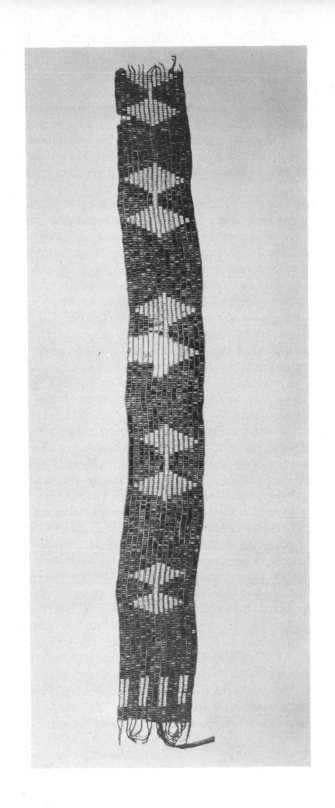

The celebrated original Five Nations wampum belt of the Iroquois (reduced).
Courtesy of the Museum of the American Indian, Heye Foundation.

"The visitors lay a stick across the benches, and place seven bunches of wampum on this, singing for some time. The curtain is then removed, and a long song follows, the wampum being carried to the mourners at intervals, a bunch at a time, and hung on another stick. The curtain is then suspended, and the mourners sing till it is once more removed. Then they return the wampum, bunch by bunch, saying, 'You said,' and repeating the words already given."

When the seventh speech had been recited, the speaker would clean the mats on which they had been sitting of the figurative bloodstains, "so that they may for a time cease to be reminded of their losses, and may regain their former cheerfulness." He then concluded with the emphatic words, "Show me the man," whereupon the incumbent chief was brought forth, and, flanked by two other chiefs, marched back and forth in the council house, while proclaiming his new name and office. This was followed finally by a reading of the wampum belts that contained the history of the League.

Hale adds: "The mourning wampum, in modern days, is left, or supposed to be left, with the kindred of the late chief until another death shall occur among the members of the Council, when it is to be passed on to the family of the deceased. This economy is made necessary by the fact that only one store of such wampum now exists, as the article is no longer made. It is probable that in ancient times, the wampum was left permanently with the family of the deceased, as a memorial of the departed chief."

Wampum belts were not used in the condolence ceremony itself, but, along with triple strings, were sometimes given as private tokens of grief. Sir William Johnson, the British colonial leader who so endeared himself to the Indians, was buried with a double wampum belt covering his body.

Wampum was also used in the happier circumstances of courtship. A special forked string was sent by emissaries of the suitor to the girl of his choice. The string consisted primarily of purple beads, but with, perhaps, four inserts of white beads, arranged as the fourth and fifth beads from each end. It was bound by a white ribbon at the top, and a dark one at the bottom.

The family of the girl reciprocated by sending a string of its own. When the proposal was accepted, they sent a "reply" string of similar size, which, perhaps, bore an additional white bead in the center and an additional dark ribbon at the top. Sometimes, as a token of affection, the family bound their reply string to that which had been sent by the suitor. However, in the event of rejection, a reply string of only about one half size was sent.

No propitiation was complete without an offering of wampum.[88] When fishing in deep water, an Indian offered individual shells, first to assure favorable treatment by the element, and secondly to thank the spirits of the fish

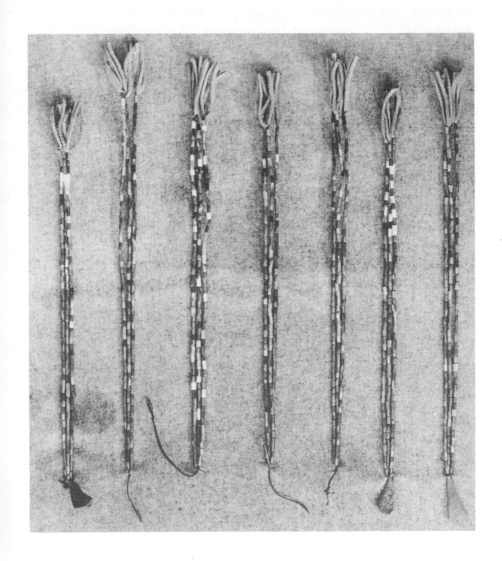

Seven triple strands of wampum (very much reduced) as used by the Onondaga in their condolence ceremony following the death of a chief.

for a continuing supply. With each new year, wampum was offered to secure the blessings of the Creator. At this time, also, the Senecas sacrificed a white dog which was adorned with a collar and necklaces of beads.

Wampum was also used in the public confessions that preceded festivals. Sometimes the wampum was passed from hand to hand, each person confessing in turn to his lapses, and resolving to conduct himself better in the future. At other times, the wampum remained in the center of the room, and those who wished to perform the duty did so, always holding the wampum while they spoke. Repentence wampum consisted of long strings, sometimes in bunches. The man who held this wampum talked directly to his Maker.

14. Wampum—Its Manufacture
and Currency Use

Purple wampum could be wrought only from the heart of the clam shell, while white beads came from periwinkle, or other suitable shells. The small white council beads were made from a smaller gastropod, or from the white parts of certain bivalves. The desirable section of the shell was broken into small pipe-shaped pieces, and these were drilled with a stone point fixed in a cane or reed, which was rapidly turned back and forth between the palms. After European contact, stone drills were replaced by awls, and palm drilling by bow drilling. The bow string was twisted around the drill shaft, and worked back and forth, causing the casing to rotate with a quick alternating motion. Beads made by the older method reveal a wide perforation, and show evidence of having been drilled from each end. By contrast, those drilled with an awl have a narrow perforation and are generally drilled straight through from one end. Finished beads were ground to a cylinder shape about one quarter of an inch long and one eighth inch wide. After being polished, the wampum was strung on fibres of hemp or on animal tendons.

Any Indian was free to make what he could, and an ambitious woman (for it was on her that the duty devolved) could mint between one and two hundred beads a day. Despite this, the demand for wampum steadily increased, and many poor white families became part time manufacturers. Almost as rapidly as the beads could be made, they were bought up by government Indian agents (first Colonial and then U.S.) and by traders who profitably employed them in obtaining furs. In this way, wampum soon acquired a general currency use.

131

It has been frequently stated that wampum did not become a currency prior to European colonization. This is not true, and, in fact, had it been so, the same logic would have to apply to the other aboriginal currencies of North America. Admittedly, in pre-contact times, most small transactions were made by barter. But this was simply because shell-money was "tight," and had to be saved for such occasions where the debt could not otherwise be settled. At various times, coins have been hoarded for similar reasons.* And even then, the wide distribution of the Indian currencies (including wampum, which, after only a few decades, circulated all along the eastern seaboard) implies a degree of ordinary commercial usage.

One occasion when wampum was always required was in the payment of blood money. The *Relation* for 1648 states:

"On the theory that putting a murderer to death would not restore life to the victim or help his friends, the Indians often received a blood atonement, which, in their words, 'covered the grave.' Among the Hurons this was not always easily made. In the *Relation* for 1636, we are told that they sometimes punished the murderer in a peculiar way, after receiving some atonement in presents. These were not then a full expiation. The corpse was stretched on poles, under which the manslayer was placed. A dish of food before him was soon filled with the decaying matter from above, and to secure its removal he must make a present of 700 wampum beads, called *hassaendista*. He was kept there at the pleasure of the relatives, and when released he made another rich present, called *akhiataendista*."

Among the Iroquois, ten strings of wampum, a cubit in length, were the value of a human life. However, in the event of compensation, twice this amount was required. The theory was that the bereaved family should not only be indemnified for their loss, but also paid for the life of the murderer, which, by his execrable act, he had forfeited. The payment was viewed as symbolical, an act of atonement rather than of compensation. Unlike the Indians of the Pacific Coast, the Iroquois believed that life was too precious to be calculated in monetary terms. Among the Huron and Iroquois, the payment was made not by the murderer, but by his relatives, village or nation. Presumably, this served as a deterrent to crime, for it heaped on the culprit the ill-feeling of his own people as well as that of the aliens.

Nevertheless, blood atonement was made only within the nation, or to another to which it was bound by treaty or solemn pact. Beyond this, neither justice nor morality prevailed. The idea of reciprocal compensations, which

* It is not an unwillingness to pay out something which disqualifies it as currency, but rather an unwillingness to accept it when offered.

one finds among the California Indians, seems to have been quite unknown in the east.

Wampum also served in ransom payments. Beauchamp describes a mutilated belt, or rather a portion of a belt that had been removed for this purpose. Anent, he quotes from an accompanying note written by Mrs. Harriet Maxwell Converse:

"Ransom belt of wampum. This belt has been divided according to the old law. If a sachem or chief was captured and condemned to die, or a murder committed, a certain amount of wampum would ransom him. In this instance the captive must have been of prominence or of national importance, as the entire belt has been divided. How much of it is missing I cannot determine positively, but as the usual length of a wampum belt is about three feet, I conclude that about one half has been taken. The diagonals of white wampum signify the tribal fires or the eight clans of the Senecas—Wolf, Bear, Beaver, Turtle, Deer, Heron, Hawk and Snipe. This belt is exceptionally rare and has no duplicate. I obtained it from a direct descendent of Mary Jamieson—the celebrated white woman captive—in whose care it had been placed by the Senecas. She guarded it till her death, when it reverted to her heirs, by whom it has been held till now—the fourth generation. It is one of the national belts of the Senecas."

Wampum was also demanded in tribute, and, ironically, the Long Island Indians, who were the greatest purveyors of the beads, were also the most heavily taxed. "The mint of wealth at their very doors," observed Woodward philosophically, "became to its possessors the source of untold misery. Constant fear kept them toiling at the mines, while the scanty proceeds of their labor only quickened the greed of their savage masters." They were forced to make large payments to both the Narragansetts and the Pequots, the latter of whom, in its turn, was mulcted by the imperious Mohawks. Woodward states that, as late as 1756, "a small tribe near Sugar Loaf mountain made an annual payment to this nation [the Iroquois] of £20 in wampum."

Nor was the White man above the sordid practice of such extortions. After 1637, the Long Island Indians, as well as others, were forced to pay an annual tribute to their English overlords for "protection,"[89] a word which, in this context, has a curiously familiar and unpleasant ring. Eight years later, the authorities, "to show their moderacon," required of the Narragansetts "but twoo thousand fathome of white wampum for their oune satisfaction,"[90] or about one hundred and twelve thousand beads. Failure to meet these exorbitant assessments resulted in stern reprisals by the English. The Dutch did not stoop to such measures, but themselves became prolific minters of wampum.

Wampum was introduced to New England in 1627, when Issac De Razier, Secretary of New Netherland, brought to Plymouth, Massachusetts, £50 in beads for the purchase of corn. From then on, there was a constant demand for wampum among the Indians of the interior. Hubbard, writing in 1801, plaintively attributed to this train of events all the Indian-colonial wars that followed:[91]

"Whatever were the honey in the mouth of that beast of trade, there was a deadly sting in the tail. For it is said they (the Dutch) first brought our people to the knowledge of wampum-peage, and the acquaintance therewith occasioned the Indians of these parts to learn the skill to make it, by which, as by the exchange of money, they purchased store of artillery, both from the English, Dutch and French, which proved a fatal business to those that were concerned in it."

The Indians measured out the beads according to a span which extended from the end of the little finger to the elbow joint. Such a unit was, of course, flexible, and the colonial authorities complained that they had always to deal with the tallest natives. In the end, the New Englanders fixed the value of the beads by count. In 1637, the Massachusetts Bay authorities ordered that six beads pass for a penny, for any sum under a shilling.[92] This referred to white beads only, the purple being reckoned at twice the amount. In the same year, Connecticut received wampum for taxes at the rate of four to the penny.[93] In 1640, each of these colonies attempted to change to the standard of the other. Massachusetts fixed the rate at four to a penny, and Connecticut briefly at six and then back to four. In 1641, Massachusetts changed back to six beads to the penny, and extended the legal tender of wampum from a shilling to £10.

In New Netherland (later New York), wampum beads were passing at four to a stiver, which was equivalent to an English penny.[94] As the result of an influx of poor grade beads, an ordinance was passed in April, 1641, forbidding anyone to "receive in payment, or to pay out, any unpolished Wampum during the next Month of May, except at Fife for one stiver, and that strung, and then, after that six beads for one stiver." Another New Netherland ordinance, this one passed in May, 1650, complained that among the loose wampum were many with holes half finished, together with others made of stone, bone, glass, muscle-shell, horn and even wood. The ordinance prohibited the further circulation of loose wampum, and fixed the rate of "poor strung wampum" at eight to the stiver.

By 1657, the amount of wampum in circulation was so great that the medium began to depreciate. Its legal tender status was revoked in Massachusetts in 1661, and similar ordinances were soon passed among the other

Imitation wampum, made of porcelain, and used for trade with the Indians.
Courtesy of the Museum of the American Indian, Heye Foundation.

New England colonies. As of 1662, white beads were rated in New York at only twenty-four beads to the stiver.

The last official use of wampum seems to have been in connection with the Brooklyn ferry. In 1693, the commuter fare between New York and Brooklyn was eight stivers in beads, or a silver two pence. Unofficially, wampum continued to circulate, and during the early nineteenth century it was once again in great demand due to the vigorous fur trading activities of John Jacob Astor.

I have already mentioned how, in early times, many of the poorer colonists took to the manufacture of wampum to supplement their regular income. The Indians, for their part, were only too happy to be relieved of the drudgery, and henceforth obtained their supply in exchange for furs of all kinds. Ultimately, however, this arrangement proved very unprofitable to the Red man. By the 1840's, when his supply of beaver and other fur-bearing animals was nearly depleted, he had lost the ability, or at least the incentive, to make his own wampum. The beads enjoyed little currency use after this time, and, whatever he needed, the Indian had to purchase directly from the manufacturer.

The doyen of the wampum minters, and the only one then producing to any extent, was the Campbell family. The Campbells had gone into the business about 1735, and, at the time of the Revolution, were the largest purveyor of the beads, operating a factory in Park Ridge, New Jersey.

Shells were obtained from various sources. First of all, there were the ships that arrived from the West Indies, carrying some five to ten thousand of the great conch shells as ballast. These could be purchased for a nominal amount, and most were sold to other manufacturers and then bought back in a semi-finished state. The conque shells served not only to make wampum, but also the "moons" and "pipes" that the Indians loved so well. In fact, it was only from the leftover pieces that the Campbells made their white wampum beads. These were about three quarters of an inch long, and were strung in lengths of a foot each. During the early nineteenth century, Campbell wampum had a wide circulation, one string of white beads passing at a "bit," or 12½¢.

For the double-valued purple beads, clam shells were needed, and these were regularly obtained from Rockaway, Long Island. In the early days, upon the arrival of a shipment of clams, the Campbells invited all their neighbors to a free outdoor picnic. The only condition was that the guests would be careful not to break the purple "heart" of the shell, from which the beads were made. Since the Campbells could not, by themselves, consume all the clams, a picnic with the neighbors proved the most economical way to empty the shells.

Another source was the Fulton market. The Campbells contracted for the entire stock of empty clam shells. Periodically, they would visit the market, cut all the purple "hearts" out of the shells, and ship them to their factory. As a rule, one such shipment contained ten to twelve barrels of "hearts."

Writing in 1844, Barber and Howe described the method of manufacture then employed at the Campbell "mint:"[95]

"Wampum, or Indian money, is to the present day made in this [Bergen] county and sold to the Indian traders of the far west. It has been manufactured by the females in this region from very early times for the Indians; and as everything connected with this interesting race is destined, at no distant period, to exist only in history, we annex a description of the manufactory. The wampum is made from the thick and blue part of sea clam shells. The process is simple, but requires a skill only attained by long practice. The intense hardness and brittleness of the material render it impossible to produce the article by machinery alone. It is done by wearing or grinding the shell. The first process is to split off the thin part with a light sharp hammer. Then it is clamped in the sawed crevice of a slender stick, held in both hands, and ground smooth on a grindstone, until formed into an eight sided figure of about an inch in length and nearly half an inch in diameter, when it is ready for boring. The shell then is inserted into another piece of wood, sawed similarly to that above, but fastened firmly to a bench of the size of a common stand. One part of the wood projects over the bench, at the end of which hangs a weight, causing the sawed orifice to close firmly upon the shell inserted on its under side, and to hold it firmly, as in a vice, ready for drilling. The drill is made from an untempered handsaw. The operator grinds the drill to a proper shape, and tempers it in the flame of a candle. A rude ring, with a groove on its circumference, is put on it, around which the operator (seated in front of the fastened shell) curls the string of a common hand-bow. The boring commences by nicely adjusting the point of the drill to the center of the shell; while the other is braced against a steel plate, on the breast of the operator. About every other sweep of the bow, the drill is dexterously drawn out, cleaned of the shelly particles by the thumb and finger, about which drops of water from a vessel fall down and cool the drill, which is still kept revolving by the use of the bow with the other hand, the same as though it were in the shell. This operation of boring is the most difficult of all, the peculiar motion of the drill rendering it hard for the breast; yet it is performed with a rapidity and grace interesting to witness.

"Peculiar care is observed, lest the shell burst from heat caused by fric-

A painting by Frank Gregory of the old Campbell wampum factory at Park Ridge, New Jersey.

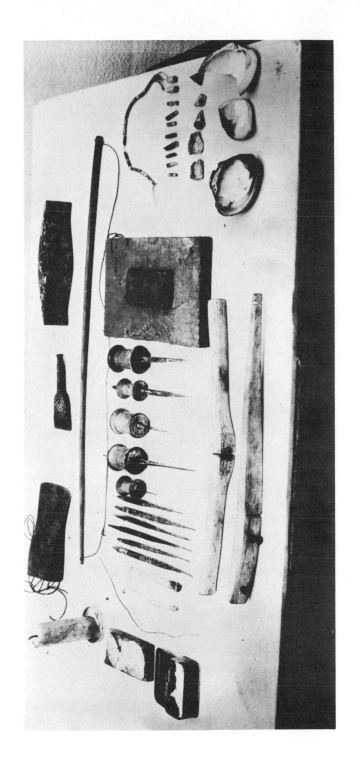

A collection of Campbell artifacts, *now in the collection of the Museum of the American Indian.*

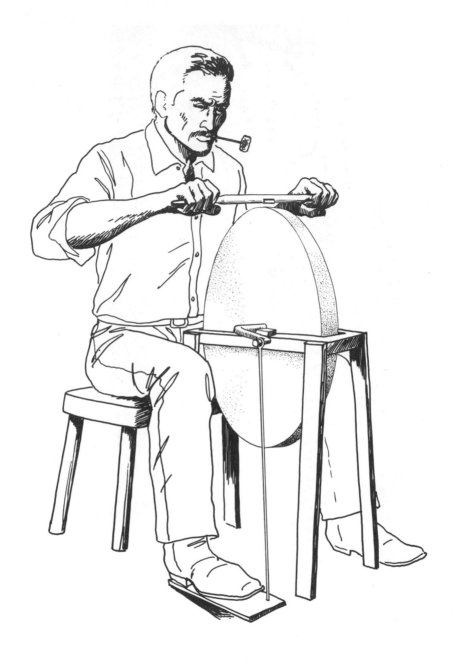

Making wampum at the Campbell "mint." The bead, held in a hickory vise, is shaped on a grindstone.

The bead, now perfectly formed, is perforated by means of a bow drill. The spindle holder rests against a breast plate worn by the worker.

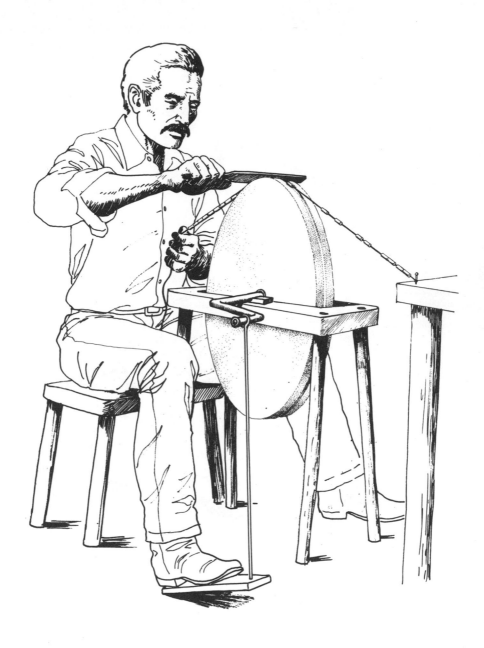

The beads, now strung, are polished on another grindstone. During the polishing, the bead is held in place by a ribbed paddle and a groove running the length of the grindstone.

tion. When bored half way the wampum is reversed and the same operation repeated. The next process is the finishing. A wire about twelve inches long is fastened at one end to a bench. Under the parallel to the wire is a grindstone, fluted on its circumference, hung a little out of the center, so as to be turned by a treadle moved with the feet. The left hand grasps the end of the wire, on which are strung the wampum, and, as it were, wraps the beads around the hollow or fluted circumference of the grindstone. While the grindstone is revolving the beads are held down onto it, and turned round by a flat piece of wood held in the right hand, and by the grinding soon become round and smooth. They are then strung on hempen strings, about a foot in length. From five to 10 strings are a day's work for a female. They are sold to the country merchants for twelve and a half cents a string, always command cash, and constitute the support of many poor and worthy families."

In 1869, James Campbell, the inventor of the family, industrialized wampum manufacture.[96] Using nothing but spare articles from around the farm, he built a machine that drilled six beads at a time. The drills were mounted in ordinary thread spools, and protruded through one end of a crude wooden rack. Opposite to them was a small metal trough, in which were fastened the shell blanks. When the drills had been brought into contact with the blanks, the entire section of the machine was lowered, by a lever, into a tank of water. Then, a crank was turned which, by means of an eccentric, moved the rack up and down and whirled the drills back and forth. The water kept the drills cool, and thus prevented the shells from bursting. It also served to wash away waste particles of shell as the drilling proceeded. Because of the unusual length of the Campbell beads, they were drilled only half way through during each operation. The rack was then lifted, the beads turned around, and the drilling completed.

The length of Campbell wampum is no doubt its most distinguishing characteristic, averaging as it does about three times that of the Indian article. This was not due to any liberality, but to the fact that wampum was now reckoned by the string, and it took less time to make one long bead than three short ones. Campbell purple wampum has a further peculiarity in that most beads trail off in white at one or the other end. By leaving a slight border around the "heart" of the shell, the minters made their stock go a little farther. It is doubtful whether the Indians of an earlier century would have suffered this adulteration, but depending as they now did on the White Man's product, they seem to have evinced no strong complaint.

The Campbell factory has been described as surrounded by white heaps of broken shells and shell dust. Within, the same condition prevailed. Heaps of shells covered the floor, and shell dust lay like white wash on benches, tools and workers. It is clear, however, that the long labors of the family were amply rewarded, for on one occasion they are said to have refused ten thousand dollars for their drilling machine. Nevertheless, it could not have been very many years after this that the neighboring Indians were removed to their reservations in the Dakotas. Thereafter, the Campbell's business languished to the point that it was finally given up. In 1905, the family made some additional beads for museums, and, following this brief resurrection, America's only wampum factory closed its doors forever.

15. North American Colonial Currencies

From the earliest days, an unfavorable balance of trade depleted the supply of coins in North America, and resulted in the circulation of various commodity currencies. These, in the merchant's vernacular, were known as "pay" in contrast to "money," and "pay as money." Money, of course, meant specie, almost all of it foreign, while "pay as money" indicated commodities that had not been made a legal tender, and were only accepted at a discount of one third off the legal price.

In New England and New York, beaver was as highly esteemed as specie, and citizens of Massachusetts were not even permitted to remove skins from the country. In New York, however, they were sometimes used in foreign exchange, as, for example, in 1661, when bricks imported from Holland were sold at $4.16 per thousand, payable in beaver skins. Bear skins were made a legal tender in Quebec in 1673, only to be supplanted, the following year, by moose skins. In backward areas like Tennessee and Kentucky, various kinds of skins continued to circulate as late as the nineteenth century.

As early as 1631, corn was made a legal tender in Massachusetts, to be received in all instances where beaver was not specifically stipulated. Three years later, however, the same colony provided that musket balls "of a full boare" circulate at a farthing each. Between 1652 and 1682, in defiance of the Crown, Massachusetts operated its own mint, but as of only eight years later, wheat, barley, corn, peas, oats, pork and beef were all serving as currencies. In Connecticut, in 1642, the General Court at Hartford provided "that no

145

man within these liberties shall refuse merchantable Indian corne at the rate of 2s. per the bushl. for any contracte made for the labor of men or cattell or commodityes after the publishing this order."

Several states which produced an excellent crop of tobacco adopted it, with varying degrees of success, as a legal tender. In Virginia and Maryland, overproduction and adulteration soon caused serious problems, and, as early as 1633, its status was nullified in Virginia. In the Carolinas, New Jersey and Pennsylvania, tobacco was only one of the many concurrent media of exchange, circulating alongside such items as wheat, corn, pork and beef, to name but a few. In New York, it shared honors with beaver, and the majority of judgments in law suits were rendered in one or the other currency.

By contrast, wool was the principal commodity money of Rhode Island, and fish and lumber of New Hampshire. In Canada, a similar economic situation obtained, with dried codfish circulating in Newfoundland, maple sugar in Nova Scotia, and wheat, corn and peas in Quebec.

We have already seen how the White man's wampum gradually supplanted that of the Indian, and how the former circulated in both aboriginal and colonial society for some two centuries. At various times, also, the colonists tried to convert the Indians to the use of European trade beads. On October 12, 1492, Columbus himself recorded:[97]

"Soon after a large crowd of natives congregated there. . . . In order to win the friendship and affection of that people, and because I was convinced that their conversion to our Holy Faith would be better prompted through love than through force, I presented some of them with red caps and some strings of glass beads which they placed around their necks, and with other trifles of insignificant worth that delighted them and by which we have got a wonderful hold on their affections."

Three days later, he added:

"A man from Conception Island was presented with a red cap and a string of small green glass beads."

As early as 1622, a factory for making glass beads was erected in Virginia, and it is probable that some of the spurious wampum about which the Colonial authorities complained originated there. The Indians, of course, were not deceived, but they seem to have liked the glass article sufficiently to use it instead of their own beads as a clothing decoration.

At least two European trade beads were adopted at different times as aboriginal currency. The first, a Russian product, is mentioned in the journals of Lewis and Clark, and concerns the Columbia River region:[98]

". . . in the evening Seven indians of the Clotsop Nation came over in a Canoe, they brought with them 2 Sea otter Skins for which they asked blue

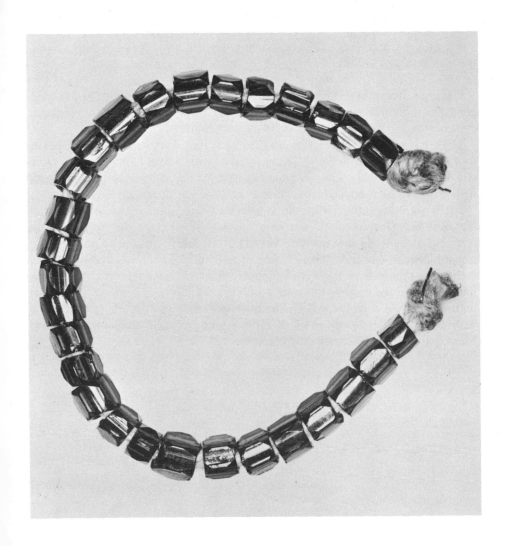

Blue cut-glass trade beads. Introduced by the Russians, these beads served as an acceptable currency on the Northwest Coast at the turn of the nineteenth century. *Courtesy of the Chase Manhattan Bank Money Museum.*

beads &c and such high prices that we were unable to purchase them without reducing our Small Stock of Merchandize, on which we depended for Subsistance on our return up this river. Mearly to try the Indian who had one of those Skins, I offered him my Watch, handkerchief, a bunch of red beads and a dollar of the American coin, all of which he refused and demanded '*ti-a-co-mo-shack*' which is *Chief beads* and the most common blue beads, but fiew of which we have at this time."

A little over a half century later, however, the cut-glass blue beads were good for nothing but decoration, and we have mention of a different bead currency in and around the Yukon.[99]

"To be accounted a chief among the Kutchin a man must possess beads to the amount of 200 beavers. The standard beads and the one of most value is a large one of white enamel which is manufactured in Italy only and can with difficulty be produced from thence in sufficient quantities."

It is with this intrusion by the White man into aboriginal economics that we must bring our own account to a close. And yet, for the time being at least, the story itself goes on. The "sweat of the sun," still settles our international balances, while the "tears of the moon" fill a part of our half dollars to satisfy the demands of the silver mining interests. Our debts to the past are manifold, and we cannot, however much we try, altogether efface them. Let us then, like the disappointed Omar, take our cash and depart, remembering with gratitude those early users of money who, in their own way, provided Mankind with one of its greatest conveniences.

*   *   *

Sources Cited

1. Lommel, Andreas. *The World of the Early Hunters.* London: Evelyn, Adams & MacKay, Ltd., 1967.

2. Diaz, Bernal, del Castillo. *The Discovery of Mexico,* trans. and ed. by A.P. Maudslay. New York: Farrar, Straus & Giroux, Inc., 1956.

3. Nutall, Zelia. "Chalchihuitl in Ancient Mexico," A paper read before the Anthropological Society of Washington, April 23, 1901.

4. Cortes, Hernan. *Letters of Cortes,* trans. by Francis Augustus MacNutt. New York and London: G.P. Putnam's Sons, 1909.

5. Sahagun, Bernadino de. *History of Ancient Mexico,* trans. by Fanny R. Bandelier. Nashville, Tenn.: Fisk University Press, 1932.

6. *Codex Mendoza,* trans. and ed. by James Cooper Clark, London: Waterlow & Sons, 1938.

7. Landa, Diego de. *Relacion de las cosas de Yucatan,* ed. with notes by A.M. Tozzer. Cambridge, Mass.: Papers of the Peabody Museum, Vol. 18, 1941.

8. Prescott, William H. *History of the Conquest of Mexico.* New York: Harper & brothers, 1843.

9. Bancroft, H.H. *The Native Races of the Pacific States.* New York: D. Appleton & Co., 1874-76.

10. Brasseur de Bourbourg. *Voyage sur l'Isthme de Tehuantepec.* Paris: 1862.

11. Valentini, Philipp, J.J. *Mexican Copper Tools,* trans. by Stephen Salisbury, Jr. Worcester, Mass.: C. Hamilton, 1880.

12. Quoted by Von Hagen, Victor W. *The Aztec: Man and Tribe.* New York: Mentor Books, 1961.

13-15. Landa, Diego de. See Ref. no. 7, *Op. Cit.*

16. Einzig, Paul. *Primitive Money.* London: Eyre & Spottiswoode, 1948.

17. Torquemada, Juan de. *Los Veinte i un Libros Rituales i Monarchia Indiana.* Madrid: 1723.

18. Pradeau, Alberto F. *Numismatic History of Mexico from the Pre-Columbian epoch to 1823.* Los Angeles: 1938.

19. Quiggen, A. Hingston. *A Survey of Primitive Money.* London: Methuen & Co., Ltd., 1949.

20. Dupaix, Guillelmo. *Antiquités Mexicaines.* Paris 1834-36.

21. Landa, Diego de. See Ref. no. 7, *Op. Cit.*

22. Martyr, D'Anghera, Peter. *De Orbe Novo,* trans. and ed. by F.A. MacNutt. New York and London: 1912.

23. Schomburgk, R. *Travels in British Guiana during the years 1840-1844.* Leipzig: 1848.

24. Ralegh, Sir Walter. *The Discovery of Guiana,* edited by V.T. Harlow. London: Argonaut Press, 1928.

25. Loven, Sven. *Origins of Tanian Culture, West Indes.* Goteborg: 1935.

26. Wisdom, Charles. *The Chorti Indians of Guatemala.* University of Chicago Press, 1940.

27. Redfield, Robert, and Villa, Alphonso. *Chan Kom—A Maya Village.* Washington: Carnegie Institution, Publ. no. 448, 1934.

28. *The Washington Globe,* editorial, Dec. 25, 1849.

29. Kendall, G.W. *Narrative of the Texan Sante Fé Exposition.* New York: Harper & Bros., 1844.

30. Smyth, William, & Lowe, Fred. *Narrative of a Journey from Lima to Para.* London: 1836.

31. Cieza de Leon, Pedro de, *The Travels of Pedro de Cieza de Léon,* trans. by Harriet de Onis. Norman: University of Oklahoma Press, 1959.

32. Acosta, José de. *The Naturall and Morall Historie of the East and West Indies.* London, 1604.

33. Up de Graff, F.W. *Head Hunters of the Amazon.* London: Herbert Jenkins Ltd., 1923.

34. Grubb, W.B. *An Unknown People in an Unknown Land.* London: Seeley & Co., Ltd., 1911.

35. Collier, John, Jr., & Buitron, Anibal. *The Awakening Valley.* University of Chicago Press, 1949.

36. Freire, Felisbello, *Historia Constitucional de Republica des Estados Unidos de Brasil.* Rio de Janeiro: 1894.

37. Levene, Ricardo. *A History of Argentina.* Chapel Hill: University of North Carolina Press, 1937.

38. Barclay, W.S. *The Land of Magellan.* London: Methuen & Co., Ltd., 1926.

39. Chalmers, Robert. *A History of Currency in the British Colonies.* London: 1893.

40. Longinos Martinez, José. *California in 1792, the Expedition of José Longinos Martinez,* trans. by Lesley Byrd Simpson. San Marino, Calif.: Huntington Library Publications, 1938.

41. Loeb, Edwin M. *Pomo Folkways.* Berkeley: University of California Press, 1926.

42. Powers, Stephen. *The Northern California Indians.* San Francisco: 1872-74.

43. Stearns, R.E.C. *Ethnoconchology: a Study of Primitive Money.* Washington: Govt Printing Office, 1889.

44. Kroeber, A.L. "Handbook of the Indians of California," Washington: *Bulletin of the Bureau of American Ethnology,* No. 78, 1925.

45. Barrett, S.A. "Pomo Myths," *Bulletin of the Public Museum of the City of Milwaukee,* No. 15, 1933.

46. Dixon, R.B. "The Shasta," New York: *Bulletin of the American Museum of Natural History,* Vol. XVII, part 5, 1907.

47. Orchard, William C. "A Pomo Headdress," New York: *Indian Notes,* Vol. 4, No. 2, Museum of the American Indian, 1927.

48. Kroeber, A.L. "Notes on Obsidian Blades," *American Anthropologist,* Vol. 7, 1905.

49. Kroeber, A.L. "Law of the Yurok Indians," *International Congress of Americanists Proceedings,* Sept. 1926.

50. Thompson, Mrs. Lucy. *To the American Indian.* Eureka, Calif.: 1916.

51. Dunn, John. *A History of the Oregon Territory.* London: Edward & Hughes, 1884.

52. Jewett, John R. *A Narrative of the Adventures & Sufferings of John R. Jewett.* Middletown, Conn.: 1815.

53. Kane, Paul. *Wanderings of an Artist Among the Indians of North America.* London: Longman, Brown, Green, Longmans and Roberts, 1859.

54. Lord, J.K. *The Naturalist in Vancouver Island and British Columbia.* London: R. Bentley, 1866.

55. Grant, W.C. *Description of Vancouver Island by its First Colonist.* London: W. Clowes & Sons, 1857.

56. Richardson, John. *Arctic Searching Expedition; A Journal of a Boat Voyage through Rupert's Island and the Arctic Sea.* London: 1851.

57. Krause, Aurel. *The Tlingit Indians,* trans. by Erna Gunther. Seattle: University of Washington Press, 1956.

58. Mobery, Henry J. *When Fur Was King.* London: J.M. Dent & Co., Ltd., 1929.

59. *The Vinland Sagas, the Norse Discovery of America,* trans. and ed. by Magnus Magnusson and Hermann Pálsson. Baltimore: Penguin Books, 1965.

60. Kotzebue, Otto Von. *A New Voyage Round the World, 1823-6.* London: 1830.

61. Boas, Frank. "The Social Organization and the Secret Societies of the Kwakiutl Indians," Washington: *Report of The United States National Museum,* 1895.

62. Lisiansky, Urey. *A Voyage Around the World 1803, 1804, 1805, 1806.* London: 1814.

63. Matthews, Washington. *Ethnography and Philology of the Hidatsa Indians.* Washington: U.S. Geological Survey of the territories. Misc. Publications, 1877.

64. Balfour, H. "Note on the Use of Elk Teeth as Money," *J.A.I.* XIX, 1890; Quoted by Quiggen, see Ref. 18, *Op. Cit.*

65. Mason, J.A. "Collection from the Crow Indians," *Museum Journal,* Univ. of Penn. XVII, 1926; Quoted by Quiggen, *Op. Cit.*

66. Stuck, Hudson. *Ten Thousand Miles With a Dog Sledge.* New York: C. Scribner's Sons, 1914.

67. Strachey, William. "The Historie of Travaile into Virginia Britannia, etc." *Hakluyt Soc. Publ.,* Vol. 6, 1849.

68. Lawson, Jno. *A New Voyage to Carolina.* London: 1709.

69. Beverley, Robert. *History of Virginia.* London: 1722.

70. Woodward, Ashbel. *Wampum.* Albany: 1880.

71. Slotkin, J.S., and Schmidt, Karl. "Studies in Wampum," *American Anthropologist,* 1949.

72. *Handbook of the American Indians, North of Mexico,* ed. by F.W. Hodge (1905). New York: Pageant Books Inc., 1959.

73. Morgan, L.H. *Fabrics, Inventions, Implements and Utensils of the Iroquois.* Albany: New York State Museum, 1862.

74. *The Voyages of Jacques Cartier;* Quoted by Beauchamp, see Ref. no. 77, *Op. Cit.*

75. Lescarbot, Marc. *Histoire de la Nouvelle France;* Quoted by Beauchamp, see Ref. no. 77, *Op. Cit.*

76. Charlevoix, P.F.X. *Journal of a Voyage to North America;* Quoted by Beauchamp, see Ref. no. 77, *Op. Cit.*

77. Beauchamp, William M. "Wampum and Shell Articles used by the New York Indians," *Bulletin of the New York State Museum,* Mar. 1901.

78. Hewitt, J.N.B. Smithsonian Institution news release, May 3, 1934.

79. Smith, Mrs. E.A. "Myths of the Iroquois," *Bureau of American Ethnology,* 2nd Annual Report, 1883.

80. O'Callaghan, E.B. *History of New Netherland.* New York: 1846-48.

81. Heckwelder, J.G.E. "History, Manners and Customs of the Indian Nations who once inhabited Pennsylvania." *Penn. Hist. Soc. Memoirs,* 1876, Vol. 12.

82. *Relations of the Jésuites,* Quebec: 1858.

83. O'Callaghan, E.B. *Documents relative to the Colonial History of the State of New York.* Albany: 1853-87.

84. O'Callaghan, E.B. *Documentary History of th: State of New York,* Vol. 2. Albany: 1849.

85. Paige, E.W. *Readings of the Wampums of the Five Nations and the Six Nations.* 1898; Quoted by Beauchamp, see Ref. no. 77, *Op. Cit.*

86. Beauchamp, William, see Ref. no. 77, *Op. Cit.*

87. *The Iroquois Book of Rites,* ed. by Horatio Hale. Philadelphia: D.G. Brinton, 1883.

88. Snyderman, George S. "Wampum in Iroquois Religion." *Proceedings of the American Philosophical Society,* Vol. 105, no. 6, Dec. 1961.

89. Thompson, B.F. *History of Long Island.* New York: E. French, 1839.

90. Thatcher, B.B. *Indian Biography*. New York: J. & J. Harper, 1832.

91. Hubbard, William. *Narrative of the troubles with the Indians in New England.* Stockbridge, Mass.: 1803.

92. Crosby, Sylvester S. *Early Coins of America.* Boston: 1875.

93. *Public Records of Connecticut,* ed. by J. Hammond Trumbull. Hartford: 1850-90.

94. *Laws and Ordinances of New Netherland, 1638-1674,* ed. by E.B. O'Callaghan. Albany: 1868.

95. Barber, J.W., and Howe, Henry. *Historical Collections of the State of New Jersey.* New York: S. Tuttle, 1844.

96. Storms, J.C. *The Story of Wampum.* Park Ridge, N.J.: 1939.

97. Fox, G.V. *An Attempt to Solve the Problem of the First Landing Place of Columbus in the New World*. Washington: U.S. Coast and Geodetic Survey, 1882.

98. Lewis, Meriwether and Clark William. *Original Journals,* Vol. III. New York: Dodd, Mead & Co., 1904-05.

99. Bancroft, H.H., see Ref. no. 9, *Op. Cit.*

Index

Acosta, José de, 57-59
Ahuitzotl, Aztec ruler, 21
Amazon stones, as currency, 18, 50-52
Amazons, 49, 51
Apache Indians, 17
Arapaho Indians, 15
Arawak Indians, 49, 52
Arawanili, legendary chief, 49, 52
Astor, John J., 136
Axe blades, models of,
    used as currency, 44-46
Axes, currency claims for, 2, 41
Aztecs:
    currency of, *see* Cacao, Cotton,
      Feathers, Gold, Jade
    Indian tribe, 20-24, 28, 30-32, 34,
      38-40
    market of, 22-24
    merchants, 21
    politico-economic system, 20-24
    tribute system, 21-22, 40

Bancroft, H.H., 32, 96
Bannock Indians, 106
Barber, J.W. and Howe, Henry, 137
Barter:
    defined, 13
    origin of, 14
Beauchamp, William, 111, 125-126, 133

Beaver, copper token, 93, 95
Beaver skins, *see* Skins
Beef, currency use of, 145-146
Bells, currency use of, 2, 41, 43, 53
Beverley, Robert, 107
Blankets, currency use of, 92-93, 96-99
Blood money, 83-84, 132
Boas, Frank, 98-99, 103
Bottles, currency use of, 59
Brasseur de Bourbourg, 32
Bride price, 83-84
Browning, Elizabeth B., 97

Cacao:
    currency use of, 2, 27, 29, 46-47,
      53-54
    "debasing" of, 47
    tribute, 21
Campbell wampum factory, 136-144
Carib Indians, 48-49, 51-52, 60
Cartier, Jacques, 110-112
Cattle, currency claims for, 58
Cayuga Indians, 117
Chalmers, Robert, 59-60
Charles V, 34, 36, 38, 46
Charlevoix, P.F.X., 111
Chi, Gaspar, 41
Chibcha Indians, 48
Chimu Indians, 18

155

Chinook Indians, 88, 93, 97
Chorti Indians, 53
Chumush Indians, 65-66
Cieza de Leon, Pedro de, 57
Cloves, currency use of, 58
Coca, currency use of, 57-58
Coconuts, currency use of, 55
Codex Mendoza, 2, 29, 34
Cogolludo, Diego L., 41
Coins:
    ceremonial incense, 53
    non-existence of among the
        American Indians, 24
Collier, John, 58
Columbus, Christopher, 24, 146
Converse, Harriet M., 133
Copper "T's", *see* Axe blades
Corn, currency use of, 145-146
Cortes, Hernan, 22-23, 30-32, 34, 36,
    38, 46
Cotton:
    currency use of, 60
    cloth, currency use of, 2, 29, 57-58
    tribute, 22
Coureurs des Bois, 93
Crow Indians, 106
Crystal:
    currency use of, 52
    symbolism of, 17

Dehadodao, Onondago chief, 112, 117,
    123
Dekanawida, founder of the Iroquois
    League, 111-112, 114, 116
De Razier, Issac, 134
Diaz, Bernal del Castillo, 22-23, 29-30,
    32, 34, 37-38, 44
Dunn, John, 88, 92
Dupaix, Guillelmo, 46
Durer, Albrecht, 34

Eggs, currency use of, 54
Einzig, Paul, 41, 46, 56
Eiriksson, Leif, 96
Elks' teeth, currency use of, 105-106
Enamel beads, currency use of, 148
Eskimos, 14, 16

Feather mantles, currency use of, 2, 30
Feathers:
    currency use of, 2, 15, 27, 30
    symbolism of, 18, 116
Fish, currency use of, 146
Freire, Felisbello, 58
Furs, *see* Skins

Gift-giving as an economic device, 97
Gin, currency use of, 59
Glass beads, currency use of, 146-148
Goats, currency use of, 58
Gold:
    currency use of, 2, 18, 30, 32-35, 106
    disc-shaped currency, 2, 18, 32-33
    eagle-shaped currency, 32, 34-35
    symbolism of, 20
Grant, W.C., 91
Gros Ventre Indians, 106

Haida Indians, 15, 89, 103
Heckwelder, J.G.E., 122
Hens, currency use of, 54
Hewitt, J.N.B., 112
Hiawatha, 111-112, 114, 116-117,
    123-124
Hodge, F.W., 110
Hoe blades, *see* Axe blades
Horseshoes, currency use of, 58
Hubbard, William, 134
Hudson Bay Co., 93, 96
Hupa Indians, 79-80
Huron Indians, 110-112, 132

Incas, moneyless system of, 18-20
Iron, currency use of, 58-59
Iroquois League, 108, 110-112, 114,
    116-118, 122-125, 132-133

Jade:
    currency use of, 2, 21, 27, 35-37, 39,
        52-53
    symbolism of, 15-16, 39-40
Jewett, John R., 88, 90-91
Johnson, Sir William, 123, 125, 128

Kane Paul, 90-91, 97
Karlsefni, Thorfin, 96
Karok Indians, 77, 80, 84
Kendall, George, 54
Klamath Indians, 80, 85
Kotzenbue, Otto Von, 97
Krause, Aurel, 92
Kroeber, A.L., 68, 74, 77, 83
Kutchin Indians, 91, 93, 148
Kwakiutl Indians, 97-100, 102-103

Landa, Diego de, 39, 46, 53
Lawson, J., 107
Lengua Indians, 50, 58
Lescarbot, Marc, 110, 118
Lewis, Meriwether, and Clark, William,
    146
Lisiansky, Urey, 100
Lodge Dance, 85-87
Loeb, Edwin M., 66-68
Logwood, currency use of, 59
Longinos Martinez, José, 65, 70
Lord, J.K., 91, 104
Lovin, Sven, 52

Magnesite beads, currency use of, 65,
    68-69, 71
Maidu Indians, 73
Maize, currency use of, 53
Makah Indians, 90
Martyr, Petrus, 47
Matthews, Washington, 106
Maya Indians, 15, 27, 29, 39, 41, 46,
    53-54
Micmac Indians, 96, 118
Minabozho, Ojibwa deity, 16, 112
Miwok Indians, 71
Mixtec Indians, 27
Mobery, Henry, 93
Mohave Indians, 17
Mohawk Indians, 110, 114, 116-118, 133
Money:
    defined, 13
    origin of, 14-18
    symbolism in, 15
Montanus, Arnoldus, 119

Montezuma, 21, 29-30, 32, 34, 38
Moses, 114
Museum of the American Indian,
    wampum belt collection of, 125
Musket balls, currency use of, 145

Narragansett Indians, 133
New York State Museum,
    wampum belt collection of, 125
Nezhuacoyotl, King of Texcoco, 29
Nishinam Indians, 66, 68, 73
Northwest Company, 96

Oats, currency use of, 145
Obsidian blades, currency use of, 80-83,
    85
Ochre:
    currency claims for, 17
    symbolism of, 17
Ojibwa Indians, 16, 124
Olmec Indians, 27
Omaha Indians, 15
Oneida Indians, 117
Onondaga Indians, 110, 112, 114, 117,
    122-123, 125

Pearls, symbolism of, 15-16
Peas, currency use of, 145-146
Pequot Indians, 118, 133
Pomo Indians, 66, 68, 70-71, 77, 97
Porcelain imitation wampum, 135
Porcupine quills (as a wampum
    substitute), 116
Pork, currency use of, 145-146
Potlatch, *see* Gift-giving
Powers, Stephen, 66, 71, 77, 83-84
Pradeau, Alberto F., 44
Prescott, William H., 29, 46
Purse, Elk's horn, 81

Quetzal feathers, currency use of, 2, 30
Quetzalcoatl, Aztec deity, 16-17, 28,
    30, 39
Quetzalcoatl, Ce Acatl Topiltzin, 31, 39

Quiggen, A. Hingston, 32, 46, 74

Ralegh, Sir Walter, 48, 51
Redfield, Robert, 54
Richardson, John, 91
Ridgeway, Sir William, 46

Sahagun, Bernadino de, 28, 32, 37-38
Salt, currency use of, 58
San Blas Indians, 55
Schomburgk, R., 49, 51
Seneca Indians, 110, 117, 125, 133
Shasta Indians, 77
Sheep, currency use of, 58
Shells:
    currency use of,
        abalone, 71-75, 85, 104
        arenicola, 91
        clam (disc beads), 65-68, 70,
            73-74, 104, 107-109
        dentalium, 74, 76, 78-81, 83-85,
            87-91, 104, 106
        esnurgny, 110-111
        olivella, 71, 74-75, 104
        roanoke, 107-109
        spondylus, 42
        wampum, 107-144
    symbolism of, 15-17
Shields, currency use of, 98-103
Shoshone Indians, 106
Skins, currency use of:
    Bear, 145
    Beaver, 92-94, 96, 145-146
    Caribou, 92
    Marten, 96
    Moose, 145
    Sea otter, 92
Slotkin, J.S. and Schmidt, Karl, 108,
    110-112
Smyth, William, 56-57
Soap, currency use of, 54-55
Stearns, R.E.C., 66-67
Stones:
    currency use of, 15, 50
    fetish use of, 17-18
    symbolism of, 39

Strachey, William, 107
Sugar, currency use of, 58-61, 146

Tallow, currency use of, *see* Wax
Teeth (animal):
    currency use of, 15, 105-106
    symbolism of, 17
Tezozemoc chronicle, 21-22
Thomas, Baptiste, 125
Thomas, George, 126
Thompson, Lucy, 85
Tin, currency use of, 46
Tlingit Indians, 92, 97
Tobacco, currency use of, 58-61, 146
Toltec Indians, 15, 31
Torquemada, Juan de, 44, 46
Tribute, 21-22, 40, 133
Tuscarora Indians, 126

Up de Graff, F.W., 58

Valentini, Philipp, J.J., 34, 46
Von Hagen, Victor, 30

Wampum, *see* Shells, currency use of
Wax, currency use of, 57-58
Webster, Thomas, 126
Wheat, currency use of, 146
White Deerskin Dance, 80, 85
Willoughby, William, 60
Wisdom, Charles, 53
Wood, currency use of, 59, 146
Wooden sticks (as a wampum substitute),
    116
Woodpecker scalps, currency use of, 69,
    77, 80, 83, 85, 87
Woodward, Ashbel, 108, 133
Wool, currency use of, 58, 146

Yerbé mata, currency use of, 59
Yurok Indians, 74, 77, 80, 83-84